TESTING LANGUAGE ABILITY IN THE CLASSROOM

ANDREW D. COHEN
The Hebrew University of Jerusalem

Newbury House Publishers, Inc. / Rowley / Massachusetts / 01969
1980

Library of Congress Cataloging in Publication Data

Cohen, Andrew D
    Testing language ability in the classroom.

    Bibliography: p.
    Includes index.
    1. English language--Study and teaching--Foreign
students.   2. English language--Examinations.   I. Title.
PE1128.A2C655   418'.0076   79-16219
ISBN 0-88377-155-1

Cover design by Diana Esterly.

NEWBURY HOUSE PUBLISHERS, INC.

 Language Science
Language Teaching
Language Learning

ROWLEY, MASSACHUSETTS 01969

First printing: September 1980

Printed in the U.S.A.   5   4   3   2   1

Foreword
by Robert L. Cooper

For language teachers who feel insecure about testing, and I suspect they form a majority of the profession, this little book will be welcome. It is easy to understand. It is sensible. It is interesting. While it is informed by considerable psychometric sophistication, it does not make the reader grapple with complicated statistics. Neither is it written as a comprehensive text which may tell teachers more than they want to know. Rather, it gives practical suggestions for language teachers, most of whom simply cannot, even with the best intentions, devote a lot of time to testing.

In addition to providing sensible and comprehensible guidance about language testing (surely a sufficient cause for celebration), it contains a wealth of ideas for teaching, not only because many of the testing exercises it presents can also serve as teaching exercises, but also because the book contains frequent discussions of learning and instructional strategies. The book is anchored upon specific pedagogical examples on the assumption that learning, teaching, and testing all influence one another. Because the author justifies his views by frequent references to the literature on second-language acquisition, to which he himself has made notable contributions, this book will be of interest not only to teachers but to researchers as well.

A book like this has been long awaited. It is a pleasure to have found it at last.

Acknowledgments

I am deeply indebted to Robert Cooper for his extensive and most helpful comments on the first version of the manuscript. Then my heartfelt thanks go to Ruth Berman, Eddie Levenston, Gene Brière, Elisabeth Ingram, Donna Ilyin, and Grant Henning for their careful reading of the second version, and for their detailed and invaluable feedback. Let me also thank John Oller and Bernard Spolsky for their continual support and suggestions from the moment that I first started planning the book, and for their "integrative" and insightful reactions to the manuscript. Finally, I offer a word of special thanks to the students in my Hebrew University language testing course, and especially to Jochai Coppenhagen. Their honest reactions and queries helped enormously to give the book its current shape.

Preface

This book is primarily intended for teachers of second and foreign languages, who use and create quizzes and tests while they teach. Their jobs require them to perform ongoing evaluation of their students' progress and to provide students with feedback. Often, the question on their minds is, *"Have the students learned this week's material?"* This book is also intended for test constructors, student teachers, advanced graduate students, and teacher supervisors.

There exist many fine books on second and foreign language testing. Some of these books exhaustively detail items that teachers can use to test pronunciation, grammar, and vocabulary in the receptive skills (listening and reading) and in the productive skills (speaking and writing). This has tended to be the popular way to lay out a testing book. The question I pose is, *"To what extent do teachers actually consult such books on a daily basis when planning classroom activities?"*

Another approach to testing involves focusing more on issues related to testing, such as the process of test taking. This book is not a cookbook of ready-made items. Rather, it focuses on the various features of any given test item. Thus the teacher gains perspective on the process of testing and ideas about how a test item or procedure could be composed. Using this information, teachers may design each item as they construct tests or quizzes.

The emphasis in most books on testing has been on student achievement, but such achievement tests are too time-consuming for teachers' day-to-day evaluative checks on student performance. The emphasis here is on features of tests and test items that can be combined relatively quickly for quizzes and tests.

Chapter 1 presents an overview of classroom testing, what it is all about and where its value lies. Then, Chapter 2 provides a theoretical framework for these classroom tests and quizzes.

Chapter 3 looks at the process of test taking. Analysis of the processes that students actually go through when they take tests can provide helpful insights about testing. For example, are they getting the answer right for the wrong reasons, or wrong for the right reasons? This chapter deals with the growing interest in the thought processes of a learner who correctly or incorrectly answers specific test items.

Chapter 4 sets forth the distinctive elements of quizzes and tests. Controversy still centers around whether to test for manipulation of discrete language items or to test for functional language ability through "integrative tests," i.e., tests that assess more than one point at the same time. While this book is primarily concerned with the testing of language as used in realistic, communicative contexts, it is recognized that analysis of such data often includes discrete-point approaches. This chapter analyzes the components of test items—i.e., the item-stimulus format, the item-response format, and the tested response behavior. The distinctive-element approach is offered in place of the more lengthy and more exhaustive coverage of the testing of language skills (speaking, listening, reading, and writing).

Chapter 5 takes three integrative tests as a point of departure for assessing functional language ability. These tests are (1) the cloze test, (2) dictation as a test of listening comprehension and of writing, and (3) dialog as a test of speaking. Testing not only involves selection of the best stimulus format to obtain the desired results, but also involves the scoring and evaluation of these results. Attention is paid throughout the book to the analysis of results and to the implications of these results.

It is hoped that this book will stimulate some thought about controversial issues in classroom testing, and that readers will be encouraged to deal with (or continue to deal with) these issues.

Andrew D. Cohen
Jerusalem, Israel
June, 1979

Contents

Introduction

This book will make ten key points:

1. Teachers do a fair amount of testing on the basis of intuition. Often these intuitions are excellent, but a teacher can also benefit from guidelines for classroom quizzes and tests. Guidelines for testing activities meant to complement intuitively based activities will be provided in the following areas·

- Why, when, what, and how to test, and how to evaluate a test
- How to classify a test and the items in the test
- Considerations of the nature of the test taker
- Procedures for determining where the learner is having difficulty with an item
- Procedures for combining distinctive elements so as to produce useful, relevant classroom tests quickly
- Suggestions for using several integrative tests of functional language ability

2. It can be helpful to take a good look at what a quiz consists of and at how quizzes can be used to eliminate the fear syndrome which accompanies the notion of testing in the minds of both students and teachers. This book purposely avoids involved statistical discussions, primarily because they may discourage less statistically minded teachers. Such discussions are found elsewhere (Wick 1973, Lindvall and Nitko 1975, for example). The hope is that teachers will come away from the book feeling more confident about using and exploring a wide variety of testing procedures.

3. A fruitful way of understanding what a test is composed of is by analyzing its distinctive elements—i.e., the item-stimulus and response formats, the tested response behavior, scoring and evaluation procedures, the characteristics of the intended respondents, and so forth. It may be particularly useful to look carefully at the nature of distractors

and how they function, particularly in the case of multiple-choice items.

4.   It is important to discuss testing issues such as the use of errors in testing. If testing is intended to serve a training function as well, the careful use of errors in testing may help train students to spot their own errors and to correct them.

5.   In discussing the nature of the respondent, I purposely include a number of cognitive, affective, and other variables. A classroom teacher may not consider any of these dimensions in preparing a given test. On the other hand, for a particular class of students, one or more of these dimensions may be relevant enough so that the teacher would consider some accommodation. For example, a teacher who notices that a sizable group of students appear field-dependent in their response behavior in class (i.e., distracted by irrelevant stimuli in the immediate field) may wish to design tests to check on this and to teach those students how to avoid such distractions.

6.   Even if both the teacher and the students are clear on what is being asked in a given item or procedure, the teacher may have little idea how the test is being answered. The teacher can acquire valuable information concerning what students really do and do not know through observing the process students use to answer questions. Thus the teacher is encouraged to devise means of learning about the students' process-oriented tactics.

7.   The book emphasizes the concept of a range of items from most discrete-point to most integrative. Although this is rather amorphous, it is a compromise, with the emphasis on a *continuum* rather than a *dichotomy*. The notion of dichotomy has created some confusion, particularly when close scrutiny reveals that supposedly discrete-point items are actually explicitly testing a few points at the same time.

8.   The testing format is broken down by item stimulus and item response in order to show that these two dimensions can be described separately and then combined in a variety of ways. Rather than list all possible oral, written, or nonverbal formats for item and response stimuli, I choose to focus on just a small number of sample formats which seem to be particularly useful in the classroom on a day-to-day basis.

9.   The book discusses three integrative tests for assessing functional language ability—cloze, dictation, and speaking—and the discussion is not intended as a sales pitch. In fact, a certain effort is made to point up weaknesses as well as strong points associated with these

types of tests. Perhaps the problem with criticizing innovative measures too severely is that teachers will then be reluctant to try them out. A certain psychological security is attached to traditional measures. New testing approaches need spokesmen who will support them in the face of opposition. Criticism, on the other hand, can also serve to improve the use of the instrument. Thus a critical discussion of cloze appears, intended to help improve its effectiveness. For example, there is a discussion of the use of discretionary judgment in applying the fixed-ratio technique to generating cloze tests, meant to help minimize unnecessary student frustration in taking the test.

10.   Throughout the discussion of specific testing formats, and particularly with regard to pragmatic language testing, an attempt is made to give full attention to test *results*. This focus derives from a desire to present not only sample items but also a discussion of possible answers, suggested scoring, and evaluation of the scores.

In essence, this book is intended to focus on a limited number of topics not covered in depth elsewhere. It probes the rationale behind certain types of testing procedures and gives research evidence and references to studies describing these procedures. Emphasis is placed on testing functional language ability, and formats chosen for examples are those that require a minimum of teacher preparation.

Chapter 1

The *Wh-* Questions
of Classroom Testing

Why Test?

The word "testing" sometimes frightens teachers because it suggests statistics and rigor. They are also afraid that they cannot make up tests that are fair and appropriate, particularly in the amount of time available. Tests also frighten students, partly because they are fearful of the unknown. They are also fearful about the consequences—the fear of being "put to the test," of being "exposed," and possibly of failure. Hopefully, the discussion in the following chapters will reduce teachers' fears about testing and help teachers to reduce student fears as well. The question is, "How does a teacher set realistic goals for tests and quizzes in general and for specific items in particular?" If teachers can set such goals and then make these explicit to students, this should help to allay students' fears about taking the test.

One reason for testing is to promote *meaningful* involvement of students with material that is central to the teaching objectives of a given course. Ideally, the goals of the test reflect the goals of the course, which are known to the student. The goals of tests or of test items should be clear to students so that they need not spend time second-guessing the teacher. If students spend their time searching

1

for a hidden agenda, they are distracted from the task at hand. If students perceive the test or quiz[1] as relevant to their needs in the course, they are probably going to engage themselves more actively in the process of dealing with it.

Although students often complain about having to take tests, they actually benefit from them in more ways than one. First, quizzes motivate students to pay closer attention to the material, particularly if the teacher announces at the outset that there will be a quiz on material about to be presented (Krypsin and Feldhusen 1974). Also the answering of a quiz or test serves as an inducement for students to review their materials, to get their notebooks in order, to sort out and classify grammatical rules and vocabulary, or to do whatever else particular students do to review for tests. In a nutshell, preparation for a test stimulates thought about the material.

While the test is in progress, students have an opportunity to see how well they are able to perform. This in itself is feedback, although it may well be that the students think they are doing fine, whereas the actual score turns out to be quite low. When the test has been scored and evaluated by the teacher, students have feedback concerning how well they did on what the test tested. Ideally, they learn something about their areas of strengths and about the areas where they are weak and could stand to review (Rivers 1968).

Tests and quizzes can also benefit teachers in several ways. The design and construction of a quiz or test acts as an incentive to a teacher to determine the goals of instruction:

Subject matter (e.g., pronunciation, grammar, vocabulary)

Skill (receptive—listening and reading; productive—speaking and writing)

Desired level of achievement that the class as a whole and students individually are expected to attain

Ideally, the above goals should be clear to teachers *before* they prepare the test, but in practice, preparation of a test often constitutes the incentive for teachers to ask themselves what the goals really are.

When the results are in, the teacher can see how well the students did on the material tested and check for any discrepancies between expectations and actual performance. This information may suggest how well the students are learning or have mastered the material, how well the teacher has put across the material, or just how well the item was written. Such feedback to the teacher can suggest areas for instruction or for review.

Of course, all this feedback is not automatically transferred to the teacher just by virtue of the fact that the quiz or test is administered.

Rather, teachers get only as much out of the results as they invest in analysis. It may be profitable to analyze the results on each item. For example, how many students got item 17 right? What were some of the reasons students had for producing or selecting the wrong answer? Do the results point up a weakness—in teaching, in learning, in item writing, or in some combination of all three?

The teacher can also analyze results by student, looking carefully at each student's performance on the quiz. Both items answered correctly and those answered incorrectly can help give a picture of the student as a learner and as a test taker. If teachers have examined students' answers at all, the traditional way (particularly for standardized tests) has been to do an *item analysis,* which looks at *item difficulty* (the proportion of correct responses to total responses on a test item) and *item discrimination* (how well an item distinguishes better students from poorer ones). Statistically, if only individual items are considered, reliability[2] of any given item tends to be low, and so such diagnostic information must be considered tentative.

For this reason, another approach to item analysis is recommended, namely, sitting with the student and going over the test individually, as time permits, in order to gain more precise insights into student strengths and weaknesses. More will be said in Chapter 3 about using the learner as informant in analyzing test results. Teachers may even choose to organize students into small working groups to discuss in consort the answers to particular questions—i.e., what is the best answer and why other answers are less desirable (a notion that is expanded in Chapter 2).

When to Test?

Ideally, a teacher should at all times be aware of how much learning is going on and the effects of what is taught on what is learned. Thus, a teacher tests whenever he wants to know what is being learned. For this reason, quizzes might be given during every class session (particularly at the beginning levels of instruction) or at least once every week or two. Tests, on the other hand, are often reserved for major periods, such as halfway through the trimester, semester, or academic year, and at the end of the course.

The current focus on the second language learner (Jakobovits 1970, Oller and Richards 1973, Schumann and Stenson 1974) has brought attention to the fact that there is not a one-to-one correspondence between what is taught and what is learned in the language classroom. Students may not learn what is taught at all or may learn it only partially or even incorrectly. Sometimes they learn incorrectly because they pay inadequate attention or because they do not have the proper *basis* for comprehending the material—a basis gained from coming to class regularly, doing the homework, or whatever.

Sometimes it is poorly written textbooks or teacher presentations themselves that induce what have been termed "cross-association" errors (George 1972). Such errors result when a teacher or a textbook presents two words or constructions too closely together and/or not thoroughly enough. The learner has not learned the formal and functional characteristics of the first form well enough to distinguish it correctly from the second form. Mutual interference results. Students, for example, cross-associate "I am" with "I go," producing "I am go," and "to the door" with "to the window," so that they confuse "door" and "window." It is suggested that such errors may result from one of the following: (1) the teacher's allowing too short a time between the presentation of one item and another, (2) the teacher's not assuring that the students are familiar enough with the first item when the second is introduced, (3) the teacher's switching the order of presentation of the item in review, (4) a degree of homophony between the items, or (5) the teacher's use of a common presentation situation that does not highlight adequately the difference between the items.

Other researchers have also called attention to teacher-induced errors, especially errors resulting from a teacher's incomplete presentation of some material (Stenson 1974). An example in the teaching of vocabulary is the following. A teacher introduced the verb + particle "point out" through example sentences and gestures. Students were then asked to use the new lexical item in a sentence. Next, the teacher introduced the verb "notice," and the students were asked to use it in a sentence. One student produced, "The barometer noticed that it wouldn't be fine." The students apparently did not fully understand the first form (and Stenson gives some suggestions as to why not) when they had to relate it to a new vocabulary item under drill conditions, and the result was confusion. Testing serves to pinpoint such areas of confusion that result from incompletely taught and incompletely learned material.

Since language learners are continually formulating and reformulating hypotheses about the way language works, they also need some feedback as to whether what they are doing is correct or not—whether the hunches, analogies, and generalizations they have made are correct or not. It has even been suggested that a learner really cannot learn in class without knowing when an error is made (Allwright 1975). Given, then, that learners do not necessarily learn what is taught and that they may learn what the teacher did not intend to teach (e.g., a sentence like, "The barometer noticed that it wouldn't be fine."), checks on the learning process through testing should take place frequently.

Test or Quiz?

Frequent checks on learning are often referred to as "quizzes." Frequency may mean the first or last 5 to 10 minutes of almost every lesson. The advantage of having a quiz at the beginning of class is that it can serve as a review of what was covered in the last class. It also helps students settle in to the class session. An advantage of having the quiz at the end of class is that it helps to keep students' attention level high. The particular moment for the quiz will depend on the given lesson. The important notion is testing while teaching—that testing can and should be seen as an interim activity.

The concept of a quiz, separate from a test, is not always developed in testing books. Perhaps the tacit assumption is that a quiz is not very rigorous or that it is only a short test anyway. However, the quiz has certain distinctive and desirable features. For example, it is brief and is therefore usually easier to construct and to score than a test. A quiz may relate just to the highlights of the day's assignment and class activities (Brook 1967). Its focus may be quite narrow, in terms of both the extent of coverage of what was taught/learned and the degree of variety of items and procedures. A quiz may serve to acquaint students with questions that will be on a test (Valette 1977). It can also give teachers feedback as to successful kinds of items or tasks for a given class. Also the merits of a short quiz should be easier to evaluate than those of a longer test: its very shortness may serve as an incentive for teachers to look closely at how well the quiz tested what was taught. On a longer test, the teacher may feel overwhelmed by the work involved in evaluating the items.

With a quiz format, the teacher has license either to announce the quiz or simply to give it without prior notice. If the activity is presented as low-keyed and even informal, students can adjust quite well. In other words, a quiz frequently causes less anxiety than does a test. Whereas frequent quizzes can provide feedback to improve student mastery of a new language, overtesting can produce diminishing returns—i.e., students receive more feedback than they are willing to process. The teacher must determine the necessary balance.

One problem with having a series of quizzes (in addition to the usual tests) is that they require extra teacher time, both in preparation and in correction. For this reason, some ideas about designing simple quizzes can be of help (and are thus a major focus of this book). Teachers can also benefit from suggestions for scoring procedures that are simple but nonetheless reliable.

To some teachers, quizzes are too formal. They prefer a show of hands or a nod of the head to indicate that the material is understood (and hence learned?) before they move ahead. Allen and Valette (1977) concede that teachers should not ask the question, "Do you understand?" since those who do not understand usually remain quiet because they are too shy to show their ignorance, and others who have misunderstood are unaware of their error. Yet they suggest that to check for student comprehension, for example, it may be enough to ask questions or plan activities that allow students to demonstrate whether they have understood. They suggest that the kind of informal feedback teachers get in normal classroom interaction may be sufficient:

> Teachers learn to tell from their students' reactions whether they have understood the meaning of a phrase. They can tell by the fluency and accuracy of the oral response whether the class has mastered a specified drill. (Allen and Valette 1977, p. 49)

The problem is that assessment of learning based on such informal feedback may be too impressionistic, intuitive, and even inaccurate. For one thing, cross-cultural differences among students and between students and teachers may result in teachers being unable to perceive whether students are in fact having trouble learning. In certain cultures student signals regarding trouble areas may not be at all overt. Furthermore, teachers in typical frontal instruction may dominate sessions to a surprising degree—surprising if they were to know how little each individual student actually speaks during such a session. It may be because the class is large, because certain students dominate discussions, or simply because the teacher does much of the talking. The teacher's inadvertent tendency to talk extensively is clearly one of the many motivating factors behind instructional approaches such as the Silent Way (Gattegno 1972) and Community Language Learning (Curran 1976), which attempt to put the teacher in a less frontal, more supportive, even silent role.

As we will see in Chapter 3 when we take a close look at the process of test taking, it is not easy for teachers to be top-notch diagnosticians at the same time that their minds are focused on the task of teaching. In fact, the two activities—one to teach the language and the other to assess whether students are learning what is being taught—both demand a teacher's undivided attention. It is true that in some class activities there is a close fit between teaching and assessing, but in others the two are far apart. It would be an endless task for the teacher to check every student for current processing of what has been taught. Hence the quiz has a genuine role—an explicit purpose—providing an opportunity to stop and take stock of what has been learned. The teacher who keeps a record of these periodic checks not only can provide diagnostic feedback along the way but can get an idea of student gains—i.e., when the gains took place, in what areas, etc.

In what ways does a test differ from a quiz? A test may resemble a series of quizzes put together, particularly if quizzes purposely consist of types of items that are to appear on a test. A test is announced in advance, is given every several weeks or at least at the end of each semester or trimester, and may take the whole class period or even longer to complete. If the student has had a series of "warm-ups" with quizzes, the test need not pose any great threat but rather can be welcomed as an opportunity to demonstrate what has been learned and to check up on what has not been mastered.

Perhaps it goes without saying that testing follows teaching. In other words, there is to be some teacher presentation, followed by explanation, and then practice or training *before* a quiz or test is introduced. It may be that students need some familiarization with a quiz technique even before it appears in a quiz. It first may appear as a class exercise—e.g., a cloze test (to be discussed in Chapter 5). This familiarization may actually serve more to reassure students psychologically than to improve their actual performance. It has been found, for example, that students trained in taking cloze and dictation tests perform no better than students not receiving the training (Kirn 1972).

Stevick (1976) has pointed out that a third thing to do after teaching and testing is "to get out of the way." In other words, testing enables both teacher and students to verify that competence has indeed become available as a basis for performance, but students must then have an opportunity to use what they have learned "productively." They decide when and for what purpose and with whom they will use the material that has been taught and tested. Of course, students should know that even though material has already been tested, it may still appear later on another test. And teachers may want to recycle material systematically for testing. Otherwise students may cram just for a test and then forget the material once the test is over.

What to Test For?

We are really asking, "What might we expect the *classroom teacher* to test for?" By phrasing the question in this way, we are broadening the concept of testing to include activities not usually associated with language testing in the classroom—e.g., testing for what the learner is capable of learning, that is, testing language aptitude, not usually the activity of a classroom teacher. Nor for that matter do teachers usually assess cognitive-style variables such as field dependence vs. field independence or tendency to overgeneralize within the target language vs. susceptibility to interference from native language. Neither do they generally assess personality variables (e.g., tolerance of ambiguity, extroversion, empathy) or strategies of second-language learning (Cohen 1977). This is not to suggest that such information is unimportant to a classroom teacher. Actually it can help in placement into class, e.g., what method of second-language instruction and what type of teacher students might respond to best emotionally and academically, given their cognitive style, personality, and language-learning strategies.

The reality is, however, that students often do not have the luxury of choosing among methods and teachers. These are givens. And individualized instruction is usually a supplementary, not a mainstream activity in language classes. Thus there will continue to be frontal hours and teachers will have to concentrate primarily on what to teach and how, not on which type of learner in the class would most benefit from which type of instruction at every step of the way. (More is said about the nature of the respondent in Chapter 2.) It may be that although teachers cannot cater to individuals, they can still cater to certain culturally prescribed characteristics.

If teachers do not usually test for what learners can learn or how they learn best, what do they test for? Sometimes teachers test language *proficiency,* i.e., the linguistic knowledge or competence students have in a language, or their ability to apply this knowledge functionally (see Upshur 1979 for a fresh perspective). In many cases, students enroll in a class after already having taken some sort of proficiency test. Such a test may be a local, departmental, or school test.[3]

Depending on the nature of the course, such a test may contain grammar items, reading comprehension items, vocabulary items, and the like. Sometimes, teachers do not have access to the actual test results; sometimes they do but do not review them. Occasionally, teachers review these test results at the outset to get a picture of the proficiency of incoming students. Sometimes teachers devise their own test to give at the beginning of the course to test what the student knows.

Another type of testing is motivated by the desire to determine what the student has learned: *achievement* testing. An achievement test assesses what has been "achieved" or learned from what was taught in a particular course or a series of courses. An achievement test may test a series of points separately (discrete-point testing) or all at once (integratively). It may well be that "the man on the street" will be unable to determine whether certain types of achievement tests assess general proficiency or achievement in a given course. Sometimes there are clues in that the vocabulary or structures being elicited seem to concentrate on an area signaling that it was covered in the course.

Actually, the same test given by a teacher at the beginning of a course to assess proficiency could be administered at the end of the course to assess the student's achievement. Thus a general proficiency test could be used as an achievement test. But an achievement test cannot necessarily serve as a general proficiency test, particularly if it tests a certain syllabus that would not be expected to be common knowledge to all second-language learners at that level. It is worth noting that an achievement test does not automatically become foolproof just because it has been "standardized" through pretesting, norming (i.e., acquiring reference data for appropriate groups of examinees), and the determining of reliability and validity.[1] If teachers work with standardized tests, it is recommended (Valette 1969, for example) that they take a close look at the tests, subtest by subtest, item by item, in order to see what is really being tested (beyond the elegant-sounding labels for each subtest). As will be discussed in Chapter 3, it can be useful to examine the papers of several students in detail, with the learners acting as informants, to see how good a job the test is actually doing. For instance, are the students getting items right for the wrong reasons and wrong for the right reasons?

The teacher can also test achievement through checking how well learners can use what they have learned in simulated or actual communicative contexts (pragmatic, performance-oriented testing). In such testing, a premium is placed on the student's ability to use responses that are normal and appropriate within the given pragmatic context. In other words, an awareness of the normal contextual constraints of the language is put above grammatical correctness in importance. More will be said about this type of testing in Chapters 4 and 5.

How to Test?

The best way to assess students' abilities in a second language is still a matter of debate. Some people swear by one approach, others by another. Even the seemingly convincing reliability and validity statistics on some innovative testing approach may not convince those who stand by time-hallowed approaches. In other words, testing methods that have been around a long time acquire a certain "face validity"— that is, people have come to agree that this looks like the right way to test whatever it is. In fact, teachers may choose testing methods that reflect the way they were tested as students. It is always easier to continue to use a known quantity than to switch to a new approach. This attitude has prompted testing specialists to urge that "language test development should not be constrained to production of face valid tasks"—that we should not limit test development to attempted measures of constructs found in today's theory (Upshur 1979).

Among those tests with low face validity can be found innovative approaches such as the "cloze" test (wherein students are asked to supply words systematically deleted from a passage) and dictation as aural comprehension (wherein a passage is dictated in a fashion that taxes listening comprehension and writing skills). At the same time, of course, even a more time-hallowed approach, such as the discrete-point testing of specific objectives, may be refined to a high level of specificity, as through criterion-referenced approaches to item design and scoring. Criterion-referenced testing is often characterized by careful planning as to intended student group, operations requested, and procedures for evaluation—i.e., which students will perform what behavior with what results, under what conditions, judged by what standard (Green 1975).[5] Ultimately, then, the criterion approach to testing is calling upon teachers to determine their expectations of the students with respect to the given test; i.e., whether all students will be expected to master the test, or to come to some minimal level, or whether, in norm-referenced fashion some distribution of performance, or a wide range of scores will be expected (Wick 1973).

Perhaps the best way to test in the classroom is through a multi-faceted or eclectic approach, whereby a variety of methods are used. This book is intended to give suggestions as to some of these varied approaches.

How to Evaluate the Test?

As any and all evaluation can help improve future quizzes and tests, teachers are encouraged to inspect certain aspects of the tests they construct. In some cases, such inspection may suggest that items or procedures be excluded from scoring or that the parts of the tests should be weighted differently than originally intended.

Teachers could pay attention to the following test-evaluation categories:

1. Clarity of instruction to the students—specifically, feedback from students regarding clarity as to the operations they were being asked to perform.
2. Appropriateness of time actually allotted—i.e., if the students were pressed for time, was this consistent with the aims of the test?[6]
3. Degree and type of student interest in the task—i.e., what parts of the test/quiz did the students enjoy doing, if any? Students could even be asked to evaluate the quiz/test anonymously (e.g., I found this test helpful/not helpful because . . . ; I like/do not like this kind of test because . . . ; etc.).
4. Level of performance on a class basis and by individual students.
5. Meaningfulness of data retrieved:
   Appropriateness of scoring procedures and weighting.[7]
   Ease of interpretation and evaluation of score.[7]
   The extent to which the test or quiz expresses what the teacher set out to assess.

Teachers who perform an ongoing analysis as to the effectiveness of different types of quizzes will be in a good position with respect to designing a final course exam. They will have an idea as to which approaches to assessment best tap the course goals they have been teaching. Where several teachers are teaching similar material, they could capitalize on this by designing, administering, and evaluating quizzes and tests in consort. There is strength in numbers.

A Recap

Testing should serve as a check for the relationship between what is taught and what is learned, and the teacher should also be on the lookout for errors caused by textbook or teacher presentation. As learners are constantly formulating and reformulating hypotheses about the way the new language works, they need feedback as to the accuracy of these hypotheses. The teacher also benefits from feedback on what is being learned. Testing is one way of providing systematic feedback to both these interest groups.

A quiz is an informal vehicle for frequent checks on learning and a lead up to a more elaborate test. The teacher should not rely on intuition as to whether students have learned some material, or trust student silence or complacent nodding of the head when asked whether they understand some material.

Some teachers may have means for assessing the students' cognitive style, personality, and second-language learning strategies before or during instruction. Teachers may also administer or have access to the results from proficiency tests that their students took. More predictably, teachers give achievement tests, often of the discrete-point variety, possibly with more integrative items, sometimes pragmatic in nature—i.e., assessing the use of language in naturalistic communicative contexts.

This book intends to steer the teacher away from testing isolated bits of structure toward testing integrative skills, particularly with attention to assessing functional language ability in real or simulated communicative situations.

Notes

1. The terms *test* and *quiz* are contrasted below.

2. *Reliability* refers to the accuracy with which the item is measuring what it is measuring—i.e., the likelihood that the obtained result would be replicated if the item were given again to the same students.

3. See Ilyin (1979) for an up-to-date rundown of English as a foreign language (EFL) placement tests available on the market and for information as to how scores on these tests correspond to levels of instruction (beginning, intermediate, advanced).

4. See Popham (1978) on deficiencies of norm-referenced tests for instructional and evaluational purposes—especially Chapter 4, pp. 74–88.

5. For example, it may be stipulated that 70 percent of the students in the class will be expected to write a friendly letter in the target language (the behavior), consisting of 50 words or more (the results), within 10 minutes (the conditions), with no more than

three morphological errors (the standard). This objective is stated in terms of the "class minimal level of performance." As Popham (1973) points out, there is also the "individual student's minimal level." For example, taking the example above, at what point is any individual student in the class said to have mastered the particular task of writing a friendly letter that is morphologically acceptable? What about the students who (1) cannot put 50 words on paper, (2) need 20 minutes to do so, (3) make more than 3 morphological errors per 50 words, or exhibit some combination of (1), (2), and (3)? The teacher may wish to set minimal performance standards for the individual student. In reality, teachers may give partial credit without a clear notion of how this partial credit relates to degree of mastery of the objective.

6. See Chapter 4 regarding testing for speed, accuracy, or quantity.
7. See Chapter 2 for a discussion of scoring.

Chapter 2

The Test, The Test Taker, Test Administration, and Scoring: Terms and Issues

The Nature of the Quiz or Test

The answer to the question "What to quiz or test for?" depends on the answer to the question "What to teach for?" The literature currently provides at least four major types of syllabi—structural, situational, topical, and notional (for review articles, see Shaw 1977, McKay 1978). The primary focus of the structural syllabus is the grammatical structure of the language. These linguistic structures are selected and graded on the basis of simplicity, regularity, frequency, and contrastive difficulty. The three remaining syllabi could all be termed "communicative." The situational syllabus focuses on language use in given social situations (e.g., landing at the airport, finding a place to live). The topical syllabus focuses on the interests and communicational needs of the given learner (e.g., communicating about sociological problems, bank management). The notional syllabus focuses on the semantic content of language. The aim is to ensure that students know how to express different types of meaning, grouped by communicative function (e.g., judgment and evaluation, suasion, argument, rational inquiry and exposition, personal emotions; Wilkins 1976).

More recently, a theoretical and practical framework has appeared for a syllabus integrating clearly identified linguistic features with communicative needs (Munby 1978 a). New criteria have also appeared for selecting linguistic features to include in a communicative syllabus (Valdman 1978).

Whatever syllabus or combination of various types is selected, the question arises of how to assess how well the students have mastered it. It has been suggested that teachers prepare a notebook of vocabulary and grammar points covered in the course and classify the vocabulary items according to grammatical function (e.g., noun, verb, preposition, etc.) (Valette 1977). If teachers were to prepare such a vocabulary list, they could easily add other categories besides grammatical function like topic groups, metaphors, idiomatic and non-idiomatic collocations, synonyms, and antonyms. The notebook could also list communicative functions covered in the course. The existence of such a notebook would be an incentive for the teacher to check periodically for the fit between the material covered in class and that covered in the test.

According to Valette (1977), the teacher is testing for two things—manifestation of linguistic competence (namely, breadth of knowledge and accuracy of usage of such linguistic elements as pronunciation, vocabulary, and structure) and ability to communicate. Valette suggests that a teacher should ask whether a "good balance" exists between both kinds of items. Clark (1972) has referred to the split as that between diagnostic achievement testing (i.e., tests aimed at checking competence on a number of specific linguistic elements) and general achievement testing (i.e., tests to get at functional language ability through assessing terminal language achievements, such as those involving longer spoken passages, unglossed reading texts, and stories retold aloud by students).

Rivers and Temperley (1978) distinguish "skill-getting activities" (perception of language categories, functions, and the rules relating the two; practice in producing sound sequences and in formulating communication) from "skill-using activities" (composing an actual message, conveying personal meaning). They suggest that even the tests of skill-getting items could be designed to be "pseudo communication," thus leading naturally into spontaneous communication activities. Oller (1976) goes as far as to say that tests of manipulative skills (= linguistic competence = skill getting) should be avoided right at the outset and that teachers should focus immediately on communicative events.

Although Oller advocates the avoidance of isolating linguistic elements into "discrete-point" items, some discrete-point teaching and testing is probably unavoidable. Of course, a true discrete-point item implies only one element from one component of language is being assessed in one mode of one skill. Thus, for example, teachers would be testing a discrete point only if they tested for the past-tense morpheme *ed* (an element from the morphological component) in elicited speech (the productive mode, the speaking skill). In reality, most test items combine several elements. Perhaps it is for teachers to decide what kind of balance they desire between items testing "skill getting" and "skill using." Chapter 4 looks in more detail at the nature of discrete-point items.

Describing a Question on a Test

Describing a test question intelligently requires a set of terms that are clear and mutually exclusive. In practice, terms used to describe tests are sometimes vague and closely related, and they may overlap. One hears reference to test items, test questions, testing points, testing objectives, and testing activities, and it may not be clear just what is being referred to. For example, in laymen's terms, the general intent of an item may be referred to as the point of the item, its purpose, its aim, its goal, or its objective. Which terms are actually used is probably not as important as is the idea that teachers should use terms consistently. For our purposes, "objective" will be used to refer to the general intent of an item, and "point" will serve as a term for describing every feature that the item tests for.

Thus one entry or question on a test or quiz will be referred to as a *test item,* and a sizable task (e.g., writing a summary of an article) will be called a *test procedure.* A *testing objective,* then, is the explicit intent of an item or procedure, which may be stated in terms of behavioral operations, like a teaching objective. In other words, students are to draw on their knowledge of the language and perform some operation with that knowledge—e.g., decode a word, read for comprehension, or listen to a dialog, and then, say, produce a word or write a phrase. A *testing point* is defined as any feature or form that a given item elicits.

While the objective of an item may be to test three points (i.e., features or forms) at the same time, the item may actually test one or more other points as well, however (with or without the teacher's awareness). This phenomenon therefore justifies our talking about intended objectives and the full range of points elicited by a given item.

Two other useful terms are *stem* and *distractor.* The stem of an item is the initial part—either a partial sentence to be completed, a question, or several statements leading to a question or an incomplete phrase (Valette 1977). A distractor is an alternate-response choice which is intended to attract students who do not know the right answer (rather than to mislead students who do know the right answer).

Tests usually consist of a series of items. Note, then, that the explicit objective of a relatively simple vocabulary item may actually be to test several points. For example, the student reads the word "ballot" and then "vote" and must indicate true/false whether the latter is a synonym of the former. This item tests for decoding ability and the ability to recognize synonyms. Or the learner reads the word "ballot" and then must produce orally an appropriate synonym. In this case, the explicit intent of the item is to have the student (1) read a word, (2) choose an appropriate synonym, and (3) produce the synonym orally—three distinct points. Had the objective of the item been to assess oral production of synonyms alone, the teacher would want to take into account that the reading of the stimulus would nonetheless constitute a point being tapped by that item.[1] If the students have limited reading ability and read "ballot" as "ballet," they may say that "dance" is a synonym.

Just as an item could test for more than one objective (an item testing the reading of a word and the oral production of a synonym), so one objective (e.g., producing oral synonyms) can be tested by more than one item and by more than one item type (see below and Chapter 4). In fact, some tests purposely include clusters of items all testing the same objective—e.g., three items all testing for control of tag questions in English. Items of a similar kind may also be grouped together to form subtests within a given test.

Perhaps the starting point in considering items or procedures for inclusion in a test or quiz is the enumeration of points that the item or procedure tests. Such an analysis might suggest broadening the item so that it covers more points at once (reading of questions and then the testing of morphological and syntactic accuracy in writing short paragraphs) or narrowing the item so that it covers fewer points (just reading of items and true/false questions about syntax). The important thing is to be aware of what the item or procedure *is* testing so that the results have some meaning and can be scored and evaluated appropriately.

Item-Stimulus and Item-Response Formats

Any given test item or procedure has a format for eliciting data from a student and a format for the student in turn to respond to the elicitation. The item stimulus may make use of an oral, written, or nonverbal medium or some combination of these. The same is true for the item-response format. Thus treating *format* as the joining of the medium for the item stimulus with the medium for the item response, we see that there are at least nine possible item-stimulus and item-response formats—even before considering combined formats like an oral *and* nonverbal (i.e., gestural or pictorial) stimulus and a written response (e.g., oral stimulus/oral response, oral stimulus/ written response, oral stimulus/nonverbal response, written stimulus/ oral response).

Item Type

What emerges from the combination of an item stimulus and an item response is what will be referred to as an *item type.* Thus, for example, the item stimulus may be a reading passage followed by a series of statements about the passage. The item-response format may call for indicating whether each statement is true or false (T/F). In this section, just several item types will be discussed, namely, those calling for alternate-response and multiple-choice item-response formats.

Alternate-response format

It is interesting that strong arguments have been advanced pro and con with regard to using a true/false, correct/incorrect, yes/no item-response format. What emerges is a picture that this response format can be effective under certain conditions. For example, sources specify that each statement must be entirely true/correct or false/ incorrect (Green 1975). Thus "specific determiners" like "all," "always," and "never" lead students to avoid endorsing true statements. "Sometimes" leads students to endorse true statements (Thorndike and Hagen 1969). It has also been recommended that relatively short statements with only one major idea be used, that the language be as precise as possible, and that true and false statements be of equal length (Lindvall and Nitko 1975).

It has been noted that one major virtue of an alternate-response format is that items using it are easier to construct for reading-comprehension passages than multiple-choice items (Heaton 1975). Also, the response format can be oral or pictorial so that the student is not required to read and interpret alternate responses. Thus such a format can be used with students who have minimal or no reading skills. The T/F approach also allows the teacher to generate more items from the same material than in the multiple-choice-item approach (Ebel 1965). For example, each of, say, five statements that would be used as alternatives for a multiple-choice item could form a separate T/F item. Then, also, students can answer more such items in a given time than with multiple choices (Lindvall and Nitko 1975).

Regarding the response format, Rivers (1968) suggests a three-way split for answering T/F questions—i.e., two points if correct, one point if indicates that "doesn't know," and 0 points if wrong, in order to discourage guessing. Ebel (1965) suggests a five-way split into "probably true," "possibly true," "I have no idea," "possibly false," and "probably false." This system also penalizes for guessing but allows for educated guessing on items for which the student has some basis for response (scoring: probably T/F—if correct, 2, if wrong −2; possibly T/F—if correct, 1, if wrong, 0; no idea—0.5). Ebel notes that the reliability of weighted true-false test scores is higher than with conventional T/F scoring, which has a 50 percent guessing rate—no doubt diminishing test reliability. All the same, the most common format remains dichotomous, largely because of its simplicity in scoring.

Perhaps the way for a classroom teacher to get mileage out of T/F items is to require students to state a rationale for responding that an item is true or false. In group testing, this rationale would be written either in the target language or in the native language.

For example, let us take a sentence testing skill in dealing with reference, with appositives, and with ellipsis:

While John likes to eat ice cream in the winter even if it's cold out, Tim, his good friend, doesn't.

Mark as T/F the following statements about Tim:

1. Tim is a friend of John's.   T/F
2. Tim eats ice cream in all seasons. T/F

Assuming the student gave the correct response to 1, "true," that Tim is a friend of John's, he would have to tell the group how he arrived at that response—e.g., that *his* of "his good friend" refers back to "John," and that the appositive phrase ("his good friend") modifies "Tim." Then, with respect to 2, the students may simply complete the sentence out loud—i.e., (Tim doesn't) "like to eat ice cream in the winter" (the part eliminated through ellipsis), to demonstrate that the item is false. Regardless of whether the students use the metalanguage of linguistic analysis to explain their reasoning (reference, ellipsis, etc.) or simply talk or write in simpler terms, they would be expected to indicate their awareness of the relationships described above in order to get the T/F answers correct.

Multiple-choice response format

Because it takes time to design good multiple-choice items, the format is probably not used too frequently by teachers for classroom quizzes and tests. Sometimes, in fact, this response format is viewed as a default choice rather than a preferred one where large numbers of students are being tested and there is no time to score open-ended responses. Multiple-choice items may turn up in classroom activities because such items are an integral part of commercial materials or of local materials produced independently of a particular teacher's class. In these instances, then, the items are not the teacher's own items but reflect the orientation of others.

Since multiple-choice items are an option for classroom testing, it appears warranted to discuss here a gray area with respect to constructing such items: the selection of distractors. Often the teacher chooses distractors on the basis of intuition. The problem is that a teacher's intuitions about what will "distract" students away from the correct answer are not always accurate. Bormuth (1970) suggested that multiple-choice distractors could be constructed through linguistic manipulation of "base structures." Two of the processes that he discussed were those of deriving what he calls "paraphrase transformations" and "semantic substitutes."

In contrast to Bormuth's theoretically based approach, Dobson (1974) researched the possibility of obtaining distractors for grammar and vocabulary multiple-choice items from among high-frequency incorrect answers on completion items given to students. In a study she conducted, a multiple-choice test with distractors obtained from analysis of answers to completion exercises was more reliable, *and* more difficult, when administered to 60 English as a second language (ESL) students than was a test with distractors written by two professional item writers using standard rules of item writing. The latter test was also administered to 60 ESL students of comparable ability. Let us look at some of the similarities and differences between items based on student responses and those based on the judgment of professionals.

With regard to grammar items like the following:

1) "I'm going to visit Ted today."
   "You really _____ to tell him first."

we see below that the item based on student responses included distractors related to the meaning of the stem, such as "must call"[2] and "had better," which together attracted 16 people, whereas the professionals' item used only modals, two of which attracted only three people in all:

Student-Based Choices and Response Frequencies		*Professionals' Choices and Response Frequencies*	
	N		*N*
(a) ought	− 40	(a) ought	− 43
(b) must call	− 6	(b) should	− 14
(c) might	− 4	(c) must	− 1
(d) had better	− 10	(d) might	− 2

Here is another example:

2) "That tree looks terrible."
   "The men cut off all _____ branches yesterday."

Student-Based Choices		*Professionals' Choices*	
	N		*N*
(a) of	− 13	(a) ones	− 1
(b) its	− 28	(b) of	− 16
(c) the leaves of	− 10	(c) its	− 31
(d) their	− 8	(d) their	− 12

On this item, the student-based and professional choices differ on only one distractor.[3] The professionals used the distractor "ones," which distracted only one person, whereas the student-based distractor "the leaves of" distracted 10 students. It appears that this distractor attracted respondents because of its semantic relationship to the sentence, not for its grammatical fit.

In gathering potential distractors through open-ended vocabulary items, it was found that students who answered incorrectly were prone to supply a word related semantically or associated syntagmatically (i.e., through a syntactic relationship) with a word in the item stem.

The student-based distractor (c) *bath*, in the item below, is an example of a syntagmatic associative (e.g., "sunbath"):

3) "The doctor told Penny that too much _____ to the sun is bad for the skin."

Student-Based Choices	N	Professionals' Choices	N
(a) exhibition	– 3	(a) revelation	– 2
(b) exposure	– 42	(b) exposure	– 47
(c) bath	– 12	(c) exhibition	– 5
(d) disclosure	– 3	(d) illumination	– 5

The student-based distractor "disclosure" works no better than the professionals' "revelation" or "illumination," but the word "bath" attracts a fair number *because* of the syntagmatic relationship. And finally, one more example:

4) "The clothing store will _____ its hat sale in the local newspaper."

Student-Based Choices	N	Professionals' Choices	N
(a) write	– 2	(a) advertise	– 55
(b) show	– 7	(b) circulate	– 3
(c) inform	– 7	(c) dispatch	– 2
(d) advertise	– 44	(d) petition	– 0

In this last item we see that the professionals' intuitively selected distractors were probably difficult to understand. Students might have avoided them for this reason alone. On the other hand, the student-based distractors "show" and "inform" attracted 14 respondents.

What is suggested by Dobson's research is that if a multiple-choice format is to be used, it is helpful to have some empirical basis for choosing distractors—e.g., the results of having students supply the missing vocabulary word. In fact, some standardized tests, such as Ilyin's English-Second-Language Placement Test (see Ilyin 1970), have derived their distractors for multiple-choice structure items from student mistakes. Actually, the classroom teacher has convenient sources for student-based distractors. For example, if a teacher has two parallel classes, or if two teachers have parallel classes, student answers to more open-ended questions in one class can serve as material for distractors in the other.

Another researcher tried out a series of eight theoretically based strategies for generating multiple-choice distractors for vocabulary items (Goodrich 1977). The items consisted of a stem and then choices:

5) "I write with a _____ "(a) pen
                                    (b) hose
                                    (c) book
                                    (d) fork

The study yielded a ranking of these strategies according to "potency" and "discrimination." "Potency" meant the degree to which the distractor attracted students away from the correct choice, and "discrimination" meant the ability of the distractor to discriminate or separate students at different levels of proficiency.

The relative ability of the eight types of vocabulary distractor to distract (potency) will be reported here. The rankings were as follows, with 1 being the most potent and 8 the least potent:

1. False synonyms (similar meaning inappropriate in context)
2. Contextually relevant (related to the context of the question, as in the above examples from Dobson (1974) of syntagmatic or semantic relevance)
3. Antonyms
4. Cloze-based distractors (i.e., based on answers to a cloze test)
5. Affixes (words modified by morphemic addition or deletion)
6. Graphemic variations (words with letter modified through substitution, reversal, or other alterations)
7. Arbitrary choices (i.e., words selected at random)
8. False cognates (words similar in form but not in meaning in the target language and in the student's native language, e.g., "soap" and *sopa* (Spanish) "soup").

In order to illustrate Goodrich's classification scheme, the following is an item followed by eight distractors, each representing a different category:

"He has to be careful about exposure to the sun because his skin is very _____ ."

1. False synonym: "touchy"
2. Contextually relevant: "hot"
3. Antonym: "immune"
4. Cloze-based: "thin"
5. Affix: "sensitivity"
6. Graphemic variation: "censurable"
7. Arbitrary choice: "impressive"
8. False cognate for Spanish speakers: "sensible"

correct answer: "sensitive"

Note that to call a distractor cloze-based merely indicates *how* it was developed (i.e., following an empirical approach as in Dobson's work), not what type of distractor it is. Thus a cloze-based distractor could resemble other types of distractors. In this case, the distrator "thin" is contextually relevant, referring to skin.

Thus the Goodrich approach incorporates both the Dobson approach and seven other categories to choose from in writing distractors. There are, perhaps, other categories of distractors that could be added to Goodrich's list. Goodrich has one category related to mother-tongue interference, namely, "false cognates." There could also be a category called "translation equivalence," for distractors which would represent an inappropriate second-language translation for a native-language word. In item 2 above, for instance, a distractor for Hebrew speakers could be "his," since the masculine noun for "tree" in Hebrew (*ets*) would take a masculine possessive pronoun. We could also add distractors to items 3 and 4, using the same approach. In Hebrew, the word for "exposure" (*xasifut*) also means "bareness"; so this could be used as a distractor in item 3. For item 4, the word for "advertise" in Hebrew (*pirsem*) also means "make famous"; so this could be used as a distractor.

The existence of a categorization scheme such as Goodrich's should suggest to teachers a methodology for writing multiple-choice vocabulary items. For example, a teacher could check such a list as to the potency of distractors and choose distractors accordingly, rather than simply on the basis of intuition. The use of empirically based distractors raises a theoretical issue of whether such distractors aid in the learning process or simply confuse the learner. In principle, a good multiple-choice stem will require the student to make distinctions between some material and some other material. But if distinctions are a matter of fine degrees, will the student benefit from the item?

With respect to effects of multiple-choice items, an approach by Munby (1978b, 1979) and others to the careful wording of multiple-choice reading-comprehension items deserves mention. In this approach, all or most of the distractors are somewhat appropriate, but only one is the *best* answer. And selecting this best answer calls for control of some particular "micro-skill" or combination of micro-skills. Actually, Munby sees this approach not as that of *testing* but as that of *training* students in problem solving through multiple-choice reading-comprehension questions. First, the students read a passage silently and answer a series of multiple-choice questions about it. Then they break up into groups of no more than five or six to discuss specific multiple-choice questions and to arrive at group answers unanimously or through a majority vote. The group must give reasons for rejecting the distractors in each question. Then there is a class-level discussion of the items and of reasons for rejecting the key distractors.

Let us take one paragraph from a sample passage and a multiple-choice question that would be written for that paragraph:

> The gap between East and West has also been widened by a growing discrepancy in material standards of living. Nowhere is the contrast sharper than between Americans and the people of Asia. In part because of accidents of history and geography, we enjoy a far more favorable balance between population and natural resources than do they. As a result we live on an economic plane that appears unattainable by them under existing conditions. This economic gap perpetuates and sometimes heightens the difference between our respective attitudes and ways of life. (E. O. Reischauer and J. K. Fairbank, *East Asia: The Great Tradition.* Boston: Houghton Mifflin, 1960, p. 6)

The sample question could be:

> Why does the West have a better balance between population and natural resources than the East?
>
>   (a) On account of existing conditions
>   (b) Because of an economic plane that appears unattainable by the East
> * (c) As a result of historical and geographical accidents
>   (d) Due to the growing discrepancy in material standards of living

One skill being tested is that of awareness of contextual meaning at the text level, specifically, grammatical cohesion at the within-sentence level. The adverbial clause "In part because of accidents of history and geography" is fronted. Readers must interpret the clause functionally as adverbial. Thus (c) is the best answer, but (a), for example, is also plausible. In fact, a student gave (a) as an open-ended answer to the question when this passage was used as part of a research project by Cohen and Fine (1978). However, (a) is not the best answer. In fact, it appears to answer a different sort of adverbial, namely, "when," "at what time." Answer (b) is also based on an actual student's response, and speaks to the results of this "better balance," not to its cause. In answer (d), "growing discrepancy" is simply a paraphrase of "more favorable balance," or a stating of what the condition is, not how it came to be.

We see how important the phrasing of the question is in this whole process. The question asks *why,* not *when* or *with what result.* It is then the students' task (in the Munby procedure) to arrive at just these sorts of conclusions as to why the distractors are not the best answer. Regarding the matter of plausibility, it may also be useful, at least from time to time, to use totally implausible distractors, just to see which students are not actively engaged in this reasoning process of finding the "best" answer. Such items would be unlikely to attract a lot of students, but the information as to *which* students are attracted may be useful.

The Use of Errors in Testing

There appear to be two schools of thought with respect to purposely including grammatically incorrect items as part of the item format. For example, the item stimulus consists of a sentence for which the students have to identify the grammatically incorrect element or elements, or select from, say, four underlined parts the incorrect one. Here is an example (Ingram 1974, pp. 320–321):

> Each sentence has four underlined parts, marked A, B, C and D. You are to identify the one underlined part which would *not* be accepted in formal, written English.
>
>   A   B   C
> At first the old woman seemed unwilling to accept anything that was offered by
>
>   *D
> my friends and I.

Or the respondent is given a grammatically correct stimulus for which one or more of the distractors is not grammatically correct in the given context:

> Judy didn't see Harvey yesterday, did she?
>
>   (a) No, she does.
> *(b) Yes, she did.
>   (c) Yes, she doesn't.
>   (d) No, she don't.

In this example, distractor (d) is the only grammatically incorrect response out of context. In context, (a) and (c) both involve an incorrect reply to the tag question format plus a switch to present tense, whereas past tense is called for.

Chastain (1976) warns against using incorrect language: "The students make enough errors in the classroom without the teacher contributing some of her own." He goes on to suggest that "with some ingenuity, the teacher can test the common errors without actually committing them herself" (p. 491). Ingram (1974), on the other hand, suggests that using incorrect forms in testing is perfectly acceptable. She distinguishes between teaching and testing, or between a "learning situation" and a "discrimination situation": "In the learning situation the student may have a mental set to absorb everything that is presented to him, but in a discrimination or testing situation, he has a mental set to discriminate between right and wrong answers" (p. 323).

It is interesting to note that even in teaching materials, erroneous material is, in fact, used from time to time. For example, in a section labeled "discrimination," Rutherford (1975) asked students to say "yes" if the question in a given list is grammatical, and "no" if it is ungrammatical. If it is ungrammatical, they are to say it correctly:

1. What happened?
   Yes.
2. What did happen?
   No. What happened?
3. Who said that?
4. How do we get to the post office?
5. Where you can find a policeman?
6. When do we sit down?
7. Who did ask you?
   etc.
   (Rutherford 1975, p. 31)

The scoring of student compositions in class can be both a teaching and a testing activity, depending on the circumstances under which the composition was written. The use of student errors may feature prominently in such an exercise. In fact, different methods have been proposed regarding the use of compositions with errors as a means of teaching students to write more grammatically correct compositions (Witbeck 1976). One method is to consider a single essay for total-class discussion. A second method consists of giving two students the paper of a third student and having them correct it with respect to certain points. The third method involves giving groups of two or three students a paper which the teacher has marked with guidelines or clues for finding and correcting errors. And in the fourth method, the teacher selects about five essays and duplicates them, correcting all errors except those considered relevant for class correction. Groups of students get a copy of one essay. Each individual student corrects this essay and then checks with the other members of the group to see if they agree with the corrections.

There may be a genuine place for erroneous material in checking for students' awareness of the grammatical correctness of forms. However, performance on such tasks may vary according to the type of learner. It has been pointed out that whereas adults who learn a second language in a formal situation can call upon a conscious "monitor" to determine whether forms are correct or incorrect, not everyone uses this monitor in performance. Or they just use the monitor with respect to certain rules. Even when learners are told to go back over their written work, they apparently do not catch more than a third of their errors (Krashen 1977). The same phenomenon was found with respect to errors in speaking. Three intermediate learners of English reported awareness of only 10 percent of their errors while speaking, and identified another 25 percent while listening to a taped version of what they said. In other words, only one-third of the errors they made were noticed at all (Schlue 1977).

A systematic study regarding the effects of error correction on student performance over time was conducted (Robbins 1977) as a follow-up to earlier work (Cohen and Robbins 1976).[4] In the experimental group were four university-level students of English as a second language—speakers of Arabic, Japanese, Spanish, and Persian, respectively. For one hour per week this group received special sessions on their written errors appearing in various writing tasks (e.g., speed writing in class, standard in-class compositions, and homework). A control group of comparison students received training in other skills during that time. The four students receiving the special sessions were able to locate less than a fourth of their errors, on the average, and when they did, they were able to correct only somewhat more than half of these (57 percent), on the average. Only one of the four students—the Japanese speaker—made noticeably fewer errors over time as a result of these error-correction sessions. This student was 25 years old, had been in the United States for 6 months, was a nursery school teacher in Japan, and had studied English in Japan for 10 years. This was the study pattern that she used and which yielded success: She repeated the corrected word or phrase and wrote down corrections for future reference. She often used as guidelines her own grammar rules or formulations of grammar rules that she acquired from class, from the textbook, or elsewhere. Finally, she was concerned about learning from her mistakes and worried about making careless mistakes.

In addressing ourselves to this issue of errors and error corrections, we see that while it is overly prescriptive to say that the teacher as tester should refrain from using erroneous material in testing, it is still worth pointing out that the effects of such use will probably differ according to the type of learner. Available research studies mainly speak to the possible lack of *benefits* from using errors. They do not investigate systematically the issue of whether exposure to erroneous material actually *teaches* the erroneous forms instead of the correct ones. This, too, probably varies according to the learner as well as according to the way that the material is presented (see Cohen 1975b on approaches to error correction).

The Nature of the Test Taker

Some students do well on language tests or quizzes, while others have more difficulty. What are the reasons for differences in achievement? A discrepancy between what students know and how they do on a given test may be a result of one-time performance factors, such as fatigue or apathy. Such factors should be distinguished from more enduring learner characteristics, such as "debilitating anxiety," which will be discussed in this section. A student may also temporarily lack the test sophistication necessary to do well on a certain type of test. More is said in Chapter 3 about learning how to take tests.

With respect to more enduring test-performance characteristics, learners have different strengths and weaknesses with respect to language-learning abilities, often subsumed under "foreign language aptitude." These abilities or aptitudes include such factors as verbal intelligence (the knowledge of words and the ability to reason analytically in using verbal materials), short-term auditory and visual memory span, sound-symbol associative skill (the ability to associate familiar sounds with new symbol assignments), and skill at grammatical analysis (ability to deal with new grammatical structures) (see Pimsleur 1966, Smolinski 1970, Murakami 1974). It appears, for example, that certain students have better visual memory than auditory memory, some are better at grammatical analysis than others, and so forth. This variation across students as to language aptitude will certainly have some effect on how individual students perform on particular types of tests.

A number of other factors aside from language aptitude are recently gaining greater visibility in the literature. Such factors include both strategies vis-à-vis language per se and cognitive style, personality, and attitudinal factors.

With regard to linguistic factors, learners employ strategies for simplifying the learning task—strategies often resulting in deviant forms on tests and quizzes. Such strategies include negative transfer (or interference) from the native language and overgeneralization of forms from within the target language. Students may also utilize strategies for avoiding forms or rules that they do not have complete mastery over, such as through paraphrase, topic avoidance, or appeal to authority (Tarone, Cohen, and Dumas 1976).[5] Such avoidance may or may not result in grammatical errors or inappropriate forms, given the particular context. It may be that some of these linguistic devices are used more frequently by more successful learners, though this is still very much a research question. For example, research may show that an increase in errors of the overgeneralization type and a decrease in negative-transfer errors indicates progress in learning of a second language (Cohen 1977).

Cognitive-style variables may, in fact, be closely linked to linguistic factors. For example, cognitive measures such as word-order discrimination tests, which measure the ability to *transfer* material appropriately from one situation to another, and category-width tests, which measure skill at appropriate categorization or generalization, may ultimately help predict ease at learning a second language (Naiman, Fröhlich, Stern, and Todesco 1978). The dimension of *field independence,* the ability to break up an organized visual field and to keep a part of it separate from that field, has also been related to second-language learning. It is suggested that the field-independent learner pays more attention to relevant language details without being distracted by irrelevant ones (Cohen 1977, Cohen and Aphek 1979). For example, students would say, "Quelqu'un nous *avons* raconté . . ." rather than "quelqu'un nous *a* raconté . . ." because of distraction caused by the *nous* in juxtaposition to *a* (Naiman et al. 1978, p. 76).[6] Such dimensions may ultimately provide diagnostic information about language learners that language-aptitude tests have not provided.

Personality variables may also influence how learners perform on language-learning tasks. For example, speaking fluency has been linked to extroversion among Chicano high school students in Los Angeles (Rossier 1976). Also, a four-trait factor comprising assertiveness, emotional stability, adventuresomeness, and conscientiousness related to success on a test of speaking skill in French among students in a late (grade 7) French immersion program in Canada (Tucker, Hamayan, and Genesee 1976). With specific regard to test taking itself, personality factors may work to the advantage of certain students in a test or quiz situation and to the disadvantage of other students. For example, research has shown that certain students display "debilitating" anxiety at the moment of testing, that is, their nervousness is counterproductive, whereas others may find that their anxiety actually facilitates their performance (Alpert and Haber 1960, Kleinmann 1977).

With respect to attitudinal variables, Naiman et al. found, among other things, that a student's general attitude toward the learning of a language in a particular situation (as determined by an interviewer, using a 5-point scale) was a better predictor of success on language tests than were measures of "integrative" (social) or "instrumental" (economic) motivation, two of Gardner and Lambert's (1972) principal attitudinal orientations (Naiman et al. 1978, pp. 66–67). They conclude as follows:

> a brief, but carefully designed, interview with a student may indicate a great deal more about his overall attitude towards language learning, and therefore the probability of his success, than the results of an involved attitude battery. (Naiman et al. 1978, p. 67)

The literature on testing different types of respondents has also referred to linguistic, cognitive style, and sociocultural mismatches between what the test presupposes about the respondents and what the learner actually brings to the test. Students' achievement on tests or quizzes may vary according to characteristics they possess by virtue of their membership in a particular ethnic group or culture. For instance, language tests designed with middle-class learners in mind may inadvertently cater to certain cognitive styles not characteristic of lower-class learners in a particular society. For example, it has been stated that "field dependence" is more prevalent among lower-class Mexican-American learners in the United States than among middle-class Anglos (Ramírez and Castañeda 1974). On the other hand, recent research suggests that this is not the case (DeAvila and Duncan 1978); so perhaps we need to proceed with caution before making sweeping pronouncements.

In any case, it may be an unattainable and even undesirable extreme to adjust forms of quizzing/testing every year according to the particular constellation of characteristics found in the class. However, perhaps the other extreme of continuing to give the same kinds of tests year after year without considering student characteristics is a less desirable situation. There may, in fact, be a good reason to design tests, subtests, or test items that cater to a specific population with certain characteristics. In research conducted with nonnative speakers of English attending the University of California at Los Angeles, it was demonstrated that the results of testing traditional "foreign" students were markedly different from the results for the ever-increasing group of "minority" students (Cohen 1975a). Five subtests were designed to measure foreign-like English (i.e., problem areas in English among foreign learners). These subtests included: *grammar*— multiple-choice sentence completion; *cloze* with every seventh word deleted; *reading comprehension*— series of passages with multiple-choice questions; *listening comprehension*— short-answer items,[7] a mini-lecture, and a dialog with multiple-choice responses; and *dictation*—with long phrase groups and punctuation given. The battery included three other subtests designed to tap minority-like English (i.e., an awareness of the difference between standard and nonstandard English). These subtests included: *grammar*—underlining incorrect forms in a sentence; *modified cloze*—testing regular and irregular verbs and modals; *dictation*—with short phrase groups, and graded for spelling and punctuation, with structures, spelling, and punctuation employed in the dictation based on analysis of minority student essays.

As predicted, minority students had little difficulty with the foreign-English subtests but considerable difficulty with the minority-English tests. The foreign students, on the other hand, had difficulty with the tests for foreign English but did *better* on the minority-English tests than did the minority students. The foreign students were generally more aware that certain forms were not acceptable in standard English than were minority students, probably because of the kind of English training, particularly in grammar, that the foreign students had received and their probable lack of exposure to minority forms. The students with minority-like English were found to have been in the United States for at least 4 years prior to the study, although some had in fact been born in the United States.

There are other ways in which students differ that have not been discussed here, such as with respect to the number of languages that they have had contact with and the nature of contact. For example, a learner may be a *native* speaker of, say, Spanish but actually be *dominant* in, say, English. Thus, if the output on a test of composition in a third language, say, Hebrew reflects structures which can be attributed to interference from another language, this interference may come more, or exclusively, from the dominant language (English) and not from the native language (Spanish). One study actually found more negative transfer from the *second* language (English) than from the *first* (Jamaican Creole) in the learning of a third language (Spanish) among junior and senior high school pupils in Jamaica (Lewis 1974). A major explanation given in this case was that the first language had been denigrated to the extent that it was not the language of instruction at school and its use at school was actually prohibited.

Actually, interference from a second language in learning a third language could arise even if the second language is *not* the student's dominant language. Sometimes the interference results, for example, from accidental similarities between words in the two languages. For instance, although a native and dominant speaker of English, I used a lexical item from Spanish (my third language) in speaking Hebrew (my sixth language). I chose the Hebrew word for "tickets," *kartisim,* when I meant *mixtavim* "letters," because the word for "postal letters" in Spanish, *cartas,* interfered.

Administering the Test

Procedures for administering a test may vary. For example, a test may be given in a classroom to an average-sized class (e.g., 20 to 30), or it may be given in a large hall to several hundred students. An in-class test may have an open-book or closed-book format. In a language test, open-book could mean the use of a dictionary, vocabulary lists, student notebook, and the like. It may even be an incentive to organize the notebook so that, say, grammar rules will be easily retrievable for use during the test.

The material may be tested with or without a brief review of those elements which will appear on the test or quiz. The questions may have been given to the students before class or may be presented for the first time when the test begins. A test may also be of a take-home variety, usually implying that it is "open-book"—i.e., students may consult class notes, articles, books, or whatever, in completing the test. Also, it may be that the student is not required to answer all the items or procedures on the test, but rather a subtest of these. This optional-choice approach may pertain to all or to only a part of the test.

It is noteworthy that several general books on testing speak disparagingly of open-book tests. They suggest that although such an approach may have a psychologically beneficial effect, it actually helps the bright students more and has dubious long-term benefits for the poorer students (Green 1975, Marshall and Hales 1971). *Optional* test questions are also criticized for several reasons: (1) they introduce separate criteria for rating different students (according to which questions they answered), which is likely to reduce the test's reliability, and (2) they may encourage students to learn only part of the material as well (Marshall and Hales 1971, p. 59).

The teacher may wish to reserve a special affable-but-stern posture for testing sessions in order to discourage copying. Perhaps the occurrence of unsolicited "group work" may not be of importance with regard to a quiz, but it would be worth avoiding on an end-of-trimester test. The teacher may also wish to establish some policy regarding tardiness, since a student who arrives late could use this lateness as an excuse for poor performance on the test. For the benefit of the students in general, and particularly for the latecomers, a teacher may wish to write on the board the time when the quiz/test started and when it will end, if timed (see Chapter 4 for more on speed, accuracy, and quantity in testing).

It may be advisable to give instructions and a sample item or two *before* students receive the test itself, to ensure that students will pay attention to the instructions. A graduate student of mine even recalled being asked to rewrite the instructions at the end of the grade-school exam as evidence that he *had*, in fact, read them (see Chapter 3 for a discussion concerning the nature of instructions). If there are instructions or questions to be read aloud, they should be read not only slowly but accurately as well—i.e., with no departure from the chosen wording. If the teacher does change the wording, this should be noted, since it may well affect the nature of the answers and the subsequent scoring of the answers. If questions arise regarding items or procedures on the test, the teacher may wish to paraphrase material on the test. The teacher should then be mindful as to whether such paraphrasing adds any substantive clues regarding the answer to the item or procedure. If so, it is important to pay attention to whether the whole class received this paraphrase, or just one or more of the students. Sometimes, out of "examiner fatigue," teachers may start feeding individual students just the clues they needed to answer the item.

Scoring

Scoring is often taken for granted. The bulk of the concern is given to eliciting the test data. Less attention is paid to determining the number of points that each item or procedure is to receive, and even less attention is paid to determining the *value* of the score. It is suggested in the literature that teachers develop a scoring key precisely in order to avoid the "I have a general idea what I'm looking for" approach (Krypsin and Feldhusen 1974). One good way for teachers to derive their scoring key is to take the test themselves (Valette 1977) and if possible, to have another teacher take it as well.

Scoring formats

At the most objective end of the spectrum are items using the alternate-response format: true/false, correct/incorrect, yes/no, same/different, 1 or 2. For example, a student hears one of two minimal-pair sentences (i.e., sentences which differ in only one phoneme) and must indicate whether he heard 1 or 2 (1 = The man *heats* the bottle. 2 = The man *hits* the bottle). A slightly more complex scoring procedure involves having a group of students rate whether the student being tested said the first or the second sentence. The tested student's score in pronunciation is then based on this peer rating. For example, the student says 1 ("The man heats the bottle"). Out of a class of 25 students, 19 indicate 1, and 6 indicate 2 (by raising their hands or in writing). That student's score would be 76 percent (19/25 of the students). This score thus reflects how easy it was for nonnative students to judge whether a fellow student produced the desired phoneme in a given context.[8]

Scoring could also be for the correct *ordering* of elements in a sentence—e.g., the correct ordering of elements in a question—or of correct *matching* between two sets of items. Scoring could also be checking for accurate *duplication* of material. For example, a teacher could score oral recitation for ability to stick to the text as it appears, i.e., without insertions, omissions, substitutions, or changes in word order (see the discussion of "miscue analysis" in Chapter 3). A point could be given for every word recited correctly. Perhaps half a point would be taken off for a repetition, and if readers correct themselves, they get a point added on. The main purpose of applying such rigorous scoring procedures to an activity like oral recitation would simply be to help the teacher pay more attention to the student's actual performance. Sometimes general impressions are misleading because of their imprecision, particularly if the teacher is influenced by irrelevant factors—e.g., an excellent reading pronunciation with faulty reading vs. a poor pronunciation with accurate reading.

Scoring could mean marking whether a blank has been *filled in* correctly. The scorer may wish to mark a word as correct if it is in the proper form—tense, person, number, gender, spelling—or may simply be concerned with whether the word conveys the semantic intent. For example, in:

Yesterday the girl ___*aks*___ to be excused.

the desired form was *asked*. The given form lacks the past-tense marker and is misspelled, but it does convey the notion of "asking" and so, when scoring for functional language ability, *aks* may be acceptable to the extent that attention is paid more to contextual appropriateness than to grammar (e.g., inflectional endings) or to mechanics (e.g., spelling).

At the more subjective end of the spectrum, we find general, impressionistic scoring. For example, on a given composition or speech, the teacher gives a 1 to 5 rating on each of the following: overall fluency/communicative efficacy, grammar, vocabulary, pronunciation (oral), or spelling (written). Or on a composition, a teacher could simply give a "+" if the paper is good, a " ✓ " if it is acceptable, and a "–" if it needs to be rewritten.

In order to determine whether students can get the essentials from a lecture, a teacher could score the accuracy of students' *lecture notes* from a mock lecture conducted in class. The teacher might simply check whether the student has noted the main points. More generally, the teacher could check whether a student has understood any sort of message in the target language by evaluating student feedback (an oral or written summary, answers to questions, etc.) either in the target language or in the student's native language. In a class where the emphasis is on student reading comprehension in the target language (and not so much on speaking the target language), and where all students share the same native language, the teacher may obtain a more accurate measure of student comprehension by eliciting it in the student's native language.

Student scoring

It is possible to let the students themselves score, particularly if the teacher wants them to have immediate feedback. In fact, a part of students' grades could be based on how well they score another student's paper. Valette (1977) cautions, however, that having students correct their own paper or exchange papers is "overly time-consuming" and that students make errors in scoring. She suggests that the teacher collect the papers and then review the quiz orally—by giving the students another blank copy of the quiz to take home and study. (Of course, teachers may err, too, and students are usually quick to call such scoring errors to the teacher's attention.)

In tasks like compositions, students would need considerable direction as to how to score each other's papers in order to do so accurately in the classroom. In a study which had learners systematically correct each other's compositions, Madsen (1960) found that students needed more direction from the teacher. At least one study (Witbeck 1976; see above under The Use of Errors in Testing) has looked comparatively at a series of procedures for student correction of compositions. First, the teacher/researcher tried correction by the class as a whole; one essay was selected and teacher and students corrected it together. Then he tried having groups of from two to three students work together in correcting another student's composition. In the first such approach, the group got two or three papers and had to correct certain points specified by the teacher. But even when they could decipher the handwriting, the students really did not know what to look for. In the second approach, the papers had guidelines at the margin to help students find and correct errors. Handwriting was still a problem. In the third approach, the teacher selected five or six compositions and then generated modified, typed versions such that irrelevant errors were deleted. Students within each small group were asked to correct the composition first individually and then with the other members of the group. Even in this fourth approach, with a legible copy and only relevant errors present, the level of proficiency and native-language background of the students sometimes interfered with the successful correction. Witbeck concluded that the last approach was the most successful, but he pointed out that this method did not result in correction of all the students' compositions, just of those five or six selected. So, such a technique would not eliminate teacher correction of composition outside the classroom.[9]

The meaning of the score

It was suggested above that *scoring* tests and quizzes is not the final step in the evaluation process. This is because the raw score in points does not have any inherent meaning. It is important first to keep in mind what the score comprises. For example, the score may constitute a composite of scores from several subtests or procedures. Some teachers may decide to weight different sections of the test or quiz differently. They may use, for example, one of these two criteria: "How difficult is it to get this item correct?" "How important is it to get this item correct?" The teacher may feel intuitively that certain items or procedures are more difficult. Or perhaps difficulty was previously determined empirically by giving similar items to the same or other students. The teacher then gives the more difficult items or subtests a greater point value. The teacher has to take into account that sometimes the more important material is actually easier for students to respond to. Then the dilemma is whether the teacher wants to distinguish among students through the students' ability to answer difficult items of *marginal* importance correctly or through their handling of *core* material. For example, a grammatical structure may be difficult because of its complexity, but not very important within the context of the course. The same could be said about common verb tense forms and vocabulary items. Are they central to the course or marginal?

A rather strong case can be made for not weighting items or subtests differently—i.e., for keeping to fixed-interval weighting (each item is assigned the same weight as every other item) and having the importance of the area reflected by the number of items assigned to that area rather than through weighting. Thus, in a 30-item test of vocabulary and grammar, the teacher may devote 20 items to vocabulary and 10 to grammar if the former has twice the weight of the latter in terms of instructional goals. The result is that the more important areas are tested more reliably than the less important areas (because increased number of items in an area means greater reliability).

The important point is that scores themselves are arbitrary. It is the interpretation of the scores that is the main concern. A score has meaning only in terms of some point of reference. Sometimes it is perfectly satisfactory to use the *raw score,* i.e., the score obtained directly as a result of tallying up all the items answered correctly on a test. But sometimes this number is not easy to interpret. One approach in such cases is to compute a percentage score, referring to the number of items on the test that the given student answered correctly in relation to total items on the test. For example, if a pupil receives a raw score of 28 out of 40 points, the percentage score is $28/40 \times 100 = 70$ percent.

One way to interpret students' raw scores so that they tell something about an individual's performance in comparison with other students in the same classroom or across several classrooms is to report on their relative rank within the group. The group is then referred to as the norm group, and in such cases, where the group is at the level of one or more classrooms, the norms are referred to as "local norms."

Several testing books suggest using a simple *percentile rank* calculation (Lindvall and Nitko 1975, Wick 1973)—a number that tells what percent of individuals within the specified norm group scored lower than the raw score of a given student. The procedure for transforming a raw score to a percentile rank is as follows:

$$\text{Percentile rank} = \frac{\text{number of students below score} + \text{half of students at score}}{\text{total number of students}} \times 100$$

So, let us assume that 25 pupils in the class got the following scores (ranked from lowest to highest):

59	62	67	78	87
60	63	68	78	90
60	65	70	80	92
61	65	71	84	92
61	66	72	85	93

We wish to know the percentile rank of the student who scored 72, let us say. We then count 14 students below the score, and note that there is only one student with a score of 72. The calculation is as follows:

$$\text{Percentile rank} = \frac{14 + 0.5}{25} \times 100 = 58$$

The percentile rank is 58.

We may also wish to know what the mean score was, i.e., the average score for a given group of students. To obtain the mean, we divide the student scores added together by the number of scores involved:

$$\text{Mean} = \frac{\text{sum of student scores}}{\text{total number of scores}}$$

Using the above data of 25 scores, the mean is as follows:

$$\text{Mean} = \frac{1829}{25} = 73.16$$

Thus the average score was about 73 points.

Ultimately the teacher evaluates the worth of a given raw score by affixing some sort of grade to the numbers. One way is simply to use the raw scores, particularly if the course is based on number grades and the raw score is based on 100 points. Of course, a problem here is that teachers may feel that all classroom tests must be based on 100 points—an unnecessary prerequisite. A test can easily have whatever point total emerges after desired items and procedures have been included.

Another means for determining grades is by computing percentages as described above and by letting the percentage be the grade, particularly in cases where the points on the test do not add up to 100. A third way is to convert each student's score to a percentile. If letter grades are used, the teacher may wish to determine what raw score, percentage, or percentile would constitute an A, B, C, etc. The decision as to what letter grade to give could be based on a statistically derived normal curve, but other considerations enter into the picture as well (see Thorndike and Hagen 1969, pp. 580–584, for more on grading). One way is to tally scores by interval and assign the basic passing grade to the *median interval* (i.e., the interval which includes the point below and above which 50 percent of the scores occur). If we take the above data for 25 students, the median interval is 70 to 74; so in a scoring system where a basic passing grade is 70, the scores from 70 to 74 would all be converted to 70. And then scores within each interval would be converted accordingly:

Interval	Frequency of scores	Grade
90–95	1111	90
85–89	11	85
80–84	11	80
75–79	11	75
70–74	111	70
65–69	̶J̶H̶T̶	65
59–64	̶J̶H̶T̶ 11	60

In passing, it is worth noting that the teacher may wish to score for whether the student has met one or more objectives. For example, a quiz or test may elicit five obligatory occurrences of a particular form. Then the teacher can decide how many of these forms the student must get right in order to be considered as having understood that form (e.g., 4 out of 5, or 3 out of 5). This is the "criterion-referenced" approach to scoring, wherein the score is mainly intended to indicate how many objectives each learner has mastered (see Popham 1978).

Since the students' interest is highest during and immediately after tests and quizzes, it is recommended that they receive prompt feedback as to how they did (Chastain 1976), regarding both their scores and what they mean.

Summing Up

This chapter considers the possibility that teachers keep a notebook of teaching points covered in the course syllabus. Such procedures are put in the perspective of an emphasis shifting away from linguistic competence, or "skill getting," toward ability to communicate, or "skill using." The emphasis is shifting from discrete-point testing to the testing of manipulative skills.

Terms for describing a test, such as *test item, test procedure, testing objective, testing point, stem,* and *distractor,* are defined and contrasted. It is noted that in order to discuss a test it is important to have a set of terms with which to state what the test is actually testing.

Item-stimulus and item-response formats are discussed, with special emphasis paid to alternate-response and multiple-choice response formats. It is suggested that an alternate-response format can be effective under certain conditions. It is proposed that the multiple-choice approach will be more effective if the response choices are based on more than intuition—i.e., on empirical analysis of results from open-ended questions and on the latest theoretical models in the field (e.g., basing reading-comprehension items on discourse analysis). It is also suggested that errors can be used profitably as part of the item format in testing.

Variation among test takers is also discussed. It is not just language aptitude that is to be considered, but also specific linguistic strategies that respondents employ in the learning process, as well as cognitive style, personality, and attitudinal factors.

Then, brief mention is made of ways in which the format for administering a test may vary—as through in-class or take-home tests, closed-book or open-book tests, etc. This book focuses primarily on in-class, closed-book tests.

Finally, attention is paid to the concept of a score—i.e., the format that it may take, who calculates it (e.g., teacher or student), and what it actually means. These issues are important to keep in mind as we proceed to consider the process of test taking and the construction of tests.

Notes

1.   See Chapter 4 for more on this issue.

2.   It may be that "must call" is perfectly acceptable and therefore should never have been included as a distractor (Eddie Levenston, personal communication). Thus

care must be taken so that distractors related to the meaning of the stem could not possibly fit within the context for, say, grammatical reasons, as in the case of "had better."

3.   We also note that this was a difficult item with both sets of choices in that only about half the students answered it correctly (cf. Chapter 1 regarding "item difficulty").

4.   Reports have also appeared on large-scale efforts to have students keep and review error sheets, and participate periodically in "error clinics," consisting of interview sessions with the instructor (see, for example, Sharwood Smith, 1978).

5.   It has been pointed out that students cannot *avoid* forms that they have no knowledge of (Kleinmann 1977). In the absence of linguistic knowledge, students will be forced to use some alternate means of conveying their meaning.

6.   Research with field-dependent and field-independent *native* speakers has also looked at linguistic behavior, such as the frequency of use of syntactic classes of lexical items in informal and formal written compositions. Among other things, it was found that field-dependent subjects are more inconsistent in their use of certain syntactic classes than are field-independent subjects. The investigator suggested that field-dependent persons have a greater need for "overt" syntactic structures (Henning 1978, p. 112).

7.   The student first heard ten questions and had to choose the appropriate response to each question from among alternate responses appearing in the test booklet. Then he heard ten statements and had to choose, from alternate responses supplied, the statement that the same speaker would be most likely to make next.

8.   It is also a test of the other students' ability to distinguish between phonemes, but this is part of the reason for having the entire class do the rating. The average rating should serve as an estimate of pronunciation accuracy.

9.   Since this section is on the notion of student scoring, not on the scoring of compositions per se, no attempt is made here to propose how best to score compositions. Such discussions can be found elsewhere (see, for example, Gorman 1979, Knapp 1972).

Chapter 3

The Process
of Test Taking

What Is Being Asked?

In investigating the process of test taking, we first look at what instructions are given with regard to accomplishing the particular testing task. The literature provides us with a list of "should"s associated with instructions. Instructions should be:

1. Brief, but explicit; complete and unambiguous (Krypsin and Feldhusen 1974)
2. Specific as to the form the answers are to take (possibly presenting a sample question and answer)
3. Informative as to the value of each item and section of the test, the time allowed for each subtest and/or for the total test, and whether speed is a factor
4. Explicit as to whether guessing counts negatively

In reality, classroom test items are not usually accompanied by such an explicit set of instructions. And even if they are, we are not always certain that students read and understand them. It may, in fact, be beneficial to know just what part of *oral* or *written* instructions students actually do attend to and understand, and why. Sometimes instructions are too brief, sometimes too wordy. Perhaps the teacher's reading of written instructions aloud is just so much static for certain students. Research is demonstrating to us that students are quick to perform tasks by analogy to previous tasks (e.g., Hosenfeld 1976). They may not notice a slight change in procedure from the way a task was tested previously. Thus the teacher may wish to be especially mindful of variations in response format and the need to signal them carefully to the students.

It may be a good rule of thumb to include a sample item in sections of a test where the format is not obvious. It may also be reassuring to the student to know the point value of each section of a test (and of individual items within the section if items receive different point values). Finally, suggested time to spend on a section may help students budget their time better. Thus, a section may begin as follows:

> In the following section you are to write a question for each response presented.
> Example:
>> The one in the blue jacket. (response)
>> *Which of these boys is your son?* (possible question)
>
> (25 points, 15 minutes)

Thus the section provides brief instructions, a sample item with an appropriate answer, point value for the section, and suggested time to spend on the section.

Students may not read the instructions at all. Although it is true that this may be from a lack of second-language proficiency (when the instructions are written in the target language), it may simply reflect a basic disregard for instructions as so much extra static—a hindrance in getting the task done quickly. Eugène Brière (personal communication) relates that once in the middle of an American history test for eighth-grade native-speakers of English, he inserted instructions to the effect that upon reaching that point in the test, the students were to pick up their test paper with their right thumb and index finger and give it to the instructor, while at the same time placing their left index finger on their nose, and that they would get an automatic A on the test. One out of 32 students actually performed this act, and did so most cautiously. Thus the teacher's first task is to make sure that students understand what they are supposed to do.

It may be useful to teach explicitly or at least check for students' comprehension of words and phrases that are used in instructions written in the second language. For example, students would need to perceive the precise function/meaning of "the best" as superlative if asked to select the best answer from a set of possible answers. This could be a classroom exercise in itself. The teacher provides a list of instructions, and students then have to explain what activity is to be performed or provide their own sample item.

It is always a good idea for teachers to take their own quiz or test, trying to play the role of the student respondent. Sometimes they may be surprised to find that a question which seemed to be easy to answer is actually complicated and perhaps even ambiguous. It can be helpful, perhaps even essential to have one or more other native speakers of the language take the test, particularly if it is an end-of-course exam. Such native-speaker validation can serve several functions, e.g., to identify multiple-choice items where none of the alternatives sound good, to identify ambiguous items, and to establish the upper level of achievement (Elisabeth Ingram, personal communication). Although native speakers make errors from time to time, the teacher can assume that too many "errors" from natives in general or too many errors on a particular item indicate that something is wrong. It is also suggested that the native speakers be similar in age and educational background to the second-language students for whom the test is intended.

Although it is unlikely that a teacher would wish to pilot a quiz or test on a large sample of native speakers, it should be pointed out in passing that results with natives need not *automatically* indicate that test items or procedures are inappropriate for the nonnative population. For example, Clark (1977) researched the performance of 88 native-English-speaking college-bound high school students on the new version of the Test of English as a Foreign Language (TOEFL). He found that they had some difficulty with the test, primarily with two parts of the test, Error Recognition (checking for basic points of grammar such as "parallelism of construction" and "verb agreement") and Reading Comprehension (items dealing with "passage summarization or interpretation"). He concluded that such findings need not warrant eliminating from the examination either "structure" items that the test constructor thinks are at least "subjectively indispensable" to nonnatives for effective academic work at the undergraduate level, or reading comprehension items that test developers and reviewers familiar with reading materials deem important.

The implications of this research study for the classroom teacher are that if tests are piloted at all, pilot data from a group of native speakers on a test for nonnatives can be helpful in seeing how the test works. The issue is whether a teacher should reject, say, grammar items that are not passed by educated native speakers. It could be argued that these college-bound natives from the Educational Testing Service (ETS) study would be using English in the same university contexts as the foreign students. In any event, such piloting helps to focus attention on discrete points of grammar, for example, which are controversial.

Expected vs. Actual Response Procedure: The Test Taker as Informant

It is becoming popular for teachers to approach the testing of language material from the point of view of the student going through the process of taking the test. Bormuth (1970) was one of the first to register a plea for more attention to be paid to this area of investigation:

> There are no studies, known to the author, which have attempted to analyze the strategies students use to derive correct answers to a class of items. The custom has been to accept the test author's claims about what underlying processes were tested by an item. And, since there were no operational methods for defining classes of items, it was not scientifically very useful to present empirical challenges to the test author's claims. (p. 72)

Bormuth's book outlined the objectives and major components of a theory for writing items for achievement tests, drawing on structural linguistics, semantics, and logic. Subsequently, studies began to appear that looked ethnographically at how learners at different age levels actually accomplish testing tasks. For example, with respect to a teacher's oral questioning of young children, it has been suggested that "the interrogator and respondent work together to jointly compose the 'social fact' we call an answer-to-a-question" (Mehan 1974, p. 44). On the basis of his research efforts, Mehan indicated that it may be misguided to conclude "that a wrong answer is due to a lack of understanding, for the answer may come from an *alternative,* equally valid interpretation." In other words, students may get an item wrong for the right reasons or right for the wrong reasons.

Investigating a standardized test of English reading (the Cooperative Primary Test, Form 12 A) by sitting down with individual first-grade learners and going over each item separately, MacKay (1974) found that learners did not necessarily link the stem and the answer in the same way that the test constructor assumed was correct. He determined that the test had a somewhat arbitrary frame of reference. He found that real information as to what children were using as reasoning was unretrievable from the test. He found, for example, that pictures were sometimes ambiguous. In an item requiring the student to link the expression, "The bird built his own house" to a picture, MacKay illustrates how a student chose the right picture for the wrong reason. This student chose a nest of twigs with eggs in the middle over a wooden bird house because he claimed that some big birds could not fit in the hole of the bird house. The student missed the element that people, not birds, are responsible for carpentered wooden bird houses with perches. How can a teacher avoid getting correct answers based on incorrect criteria? It helps to make the item stimulus as unambiguous as possible, but this does not rule out such behavior.

MacKay also gives an example of an item missed for the wrong reasons. The statement, "The cat has been out in the rain again" had to be linked to one of three pictures which looked roughly like these.

The student perceived the dotted wallpaper as snow and decided that this picture was of the exterior of the house. Thus, he gave the dripping raincoat as the correct answer. Once the child had perceived the wallpaper as snow and thus had eliminated the third picture, his selection of the first picture, the dripping raincoat, rather than the second, was perfectly reasonable.

The message that comes out of the work of both Mehan and MacKay is the importance of utilizing the student as an informant in order to understand better what the test is testing. Research has focused, for example, on the issue of how high school students use instructions to complete exercises in French as a foreign language (Hosenfeld 1975, 1976). Students were asked to "think aloud" on a continual basis as they did the exercises—thus obtaining an *introspective* account of what the students are doing, as opposed to a *retrospective* one, wherein the student attempts to recollect the process by which he accomplished some task (e.g., completed a test item) at some point in the past (5 minutes ago, an hour ago, yesterday, etc.).

An unspoken principle appeared to influence problem-solving behavior among these students. They seemed to ask themselves, "What is the minimal amount of information needed to complete the task?" For example, one student processed only those portions of the stimulus sentences which were essential for determining the appropriate preposition with names of places in an exercise for "reading grammar practice," e.g.:

Monsieur Abèle habite _____ Bruxelles _____ Belgique.

In other words, the student did not read the stimulus sentence in its entirety but instead just paid attention to the sections being focused on in the exercise. The student reported, "Really, all I do is check down the countries and cities and put in *en, à,* or *au* . . . I don't look at the rest of the sentence at all" (Hosenfeld 1976, p. 120).

Consistent with this short-cut matching game, a student informant revealed that she did not attend to the meaning in doing a reading-grammar task. In this task, the noun direct object was to be replaced by a pronoun such that the past participle of the verb would agree with the pronoun, e.g.:

Ils ont perdu *les bérets verts.* "They have lost their green berets."
Correct answer: Ils *les* ont perdus. "They have lost them."

The informant said that she just put *les* before the verb and added *s* to *perdu* because *vert* was masculine. She did not look at the word *bérets* at all because "you just need *les* and *verts.*" Hosenfeld suggests from this that the students may be doing something very different from what classroom teachers expect if teachers assume that the students are attending to meaning when they do such exercises.

A colleague, Edna Aphek, and I conducted a research project which included an investigation of the strategies that students use in taking an exam (Cohen and Aphek 1979). The students were American college-level learners of Hebrew ($N = 19$), on a 6-month program in Israel. After the students had taken their end-of-summer exam (9 students at the beginning level, 6 at the intermediate level, and 4 at the advanced level) marking the completion of 2 months of intensive Hebrew training, we went through each exam thoroughly and identified about 15 points for discussion with each student. These points primarily reflected types of errors we had hoped would provide insights into the strategies used in test taking. Students met individually with an investigator approximately a week after they had taken the exam, and were asked to provide a retrospective account of the strategies that they had used to arrive at various answers on their exam. Responses to these queries were content-analyzed, and the following reflects a brief discussion of some of the strategies that emerged—i.e., strategies that students themselves reported using. Hence the following discussion is not exhaustive of test-taking strategies but rather suggestive of a few such strategies.

Incomplete analysis or lack of attention

As a receptive strategy, students would not necessarily process the entire item stimulus, but only part of it, and answer that part. Our probe made it clear that students who do this are not necessarily being careless—i.e., answering too quickly or haphazardly. They may, instead, simply not understand a word or phrase in the item stimulus. The strategy, then, is to forge ahead and answer what they can on the basis of what they know. This approach is slightly different from that reported in Hosenfeld (1976) whereby students read little or none of the instructions before doing homework exercises. In that case, the students felt that they knew what to do and did not need to dwell on the question. In the current research, the student did not completely comprehend the question.

As a strategy for facilitating productive performance (in this case, writing), students would lift material intact from an item stimulus or from, say, a passage for use in an answer. The result would be verb forms incorrectly inflected for person, number, gender, or tense; verbs reflecting the correct root but an incorrect conjugation, etc.

We observed a variety of strategies for producing, say, a verb form when the rules for production had not been learned (termed "the presystematic stage" in Corder 1974). If students did not know the correct verb form, they would use the infinitive, take a form from a tense that they knew, take one inflectional ending and generalize it across person and gender, take an inappropriate tense from the stimulus and simply add the prefix for person, and so on.

Another strategy for production was simply to use prepackaged, unanalyzed material and combine it with analyzed forms. For example, given that Hebrew prepositions like *mi* "from" can be prefixed to the object of the preposition through elision (*mi* + *tsad* "side" = *mitsad*), a student learns this form as one word and then affixes another preposition to it on an exam, e.g., *bemitsad* "on from a side" intending "on a side."

Field dependence

A category related to incomplete analysis is derived from the psychological concept of field dependence (mentioned in Chapter 2), i.e., distraction from elements that are in the immediate environment but irrelevant to the language processing being called for. For example, if the learner uses a plural verb with a singular subject because the intervening indirect object is plural, this would be considered one form of field-dependent behavior. Specifically, a learner who wanted to say, "We had a new government," produced *hayu lanu memšala xadaša, lit. "were (third person plural) to us government (feminine singular) new (feminine singular)," instead of *hayta lanu memšala xadaša,* lit. "was (third person feminine singular) government (feminine singular) new (feminine singular)." Apparently the plural indirect object *lanu* "to us" distracted the student away from the appropriate singular form of the verb *hayta* "there was" (feminine singular) to the plural *hayu* "there were."

Test-induced errors

At first, it might appear that test-induced errors do not constitute student strategies, but the type of test may well influence the type of strategies that students will use. We encountered a certain number of instances where students were called upon to use their own best powers of identification, discrimination, and analogy in answering test items. They had to use their "own best powers" because they were in a situation where they could not ask for help. The instances under discussion were prompted by the teacher's introduction of unfamiliar or confusing forms.

For example, students might not discern that there is a difference between a given verb form and forms in a conjugation that the students erroneously identify it with. So, when given the form *metapsim* "they climb" and asked to give the third-person plural past tense *tipsu* "they climbed," a fair number of students wrote *metapsu. The students were probably making erroneous visual and auditory analogy to another conjugation, *hitpael,* where the past-tense form would be *hitapsu* (if it existed), as in *hitarvu* "they interfered."[1]

Use of frequently heard, popular forms

Several students reported that they would sometimes select forms simply because these were the forms that were popular; forms that they heard most often—e.g., *diber* "he spoke" when they should have used *amar* "he said"; *anašim *yisraelit* lit. "people (masculine plural) Israeli (feminine singular)" instead of *anašim yisraeliim* "people (masculine plural) Israeli (masculine plural)." These interviews with the students brought out the point that such errors as these might well not occur in natural communicative situations. However, when under the pressure of a testing situation, students may choose the initial form that comes into their heads, e.g., *diber* "he spoke" instead of *amar* "he said."

Looking for a trick

Students reported looking for the trick in a given item and trying to avoid committing the error or errors that this item was testing for. For example, when given a sentence in English to translate into Hebrew (e.g., "I want you to write a letter"), the student said that she knew there was a trick but could not remember what it was exactly. She knew that she could not use the infinitive as in English. Therefore, she used a present-tense form of the verb in the required relative clause in Hebrew. However, the tense of the verb in Hebrew must be future: *ani rotse še ata tixtov mixtav* lit. "I want that you will write (a) letter." She wrote *kotev* instead of *tixtov* (present "(you) write," instead of future "you will write").

Purposive omission

It was noted above that as a receptive strategy, students may analyze some material incompletely—i.e., deal only with those parts of an item stimulus that they understand. As a productive strategy, students may purposely omit material. For example, on one item students were asked to translate from English to Hebrew. A student reported leaving out an object pronoun because he was not sure how to say it and did not feel that it was important. The student was asked to translate the following sentence into Hebrew: "If you come to Jerusalem, I'll invite you to a party." He omitted from the main clause in his Hebrew version the object pronoun "you" (*oxta*), producing *azmin le mesiba* "I'll invite to (a) party."

Translation

Several students reported the use of translation as a test-taking strategy. One or two would write out a complete native-language version of a given text before answering questions about it. They said that this made them feel more secure. Others would at least translate questions in their entirety into the native language before attempting to answer them.

Transfer from the native language

Not so surprisingly, students would often produce forms that were inappropriate translation equivalents of forms in the native language (e.g., *be ha maslul* = "in + the + track" instead of *bamaslul* = "in-the (fused together) + track"). In some cases, students consciously indulged in interference *avoiding*—namely, trying not to choose forms that *were* like those in the native language (even where such parallels actually were correct).

Overcorrection

In some instances, students read over their tests and made changes such that the new answer was wrong, whereas the first answer had been correct. Possibly the students overcorrected because the teacher requested that they check over their work carefully. Also, students may have been too quick to assume that they probably answered incorrectly the first time since their knowledge as learners was imperfect.

* * * * * *

The results of this study suggest a procedure for helping students to improve their test-taking skills. The teacher could take the strategies summarized below and construct a short quiz where, say, one or more of these strategies is crucial for successful completion of the quiz. These quizzes would be worked through in class as part of a test-training procedure.

1. Read the directions carefully and pay attention to the entire item stimulus. Be aware that clues to the form that the answer is to take (e.g., the tenses to use, word order, etc.) are often found in the question itself. For example: Complete the response to the following questions.

    What would Billy have taken with him, had he known that it was pouring out?"

    "If Billy _____ , he _____
    _____ an umbrella." etc.

2. Pay attention to the relationship of elements to one another, and try to avoid being distracted by elements that are irrele-

vant to the task at hand (e.g., elements that suggest a different inflection from the one called for). For example: Supply the correct form of the verb for the following items as rapidly as possible.

"The list of names of all the boys in the band _____ on the dining room table." etc.

3. When having to deal with unfamiliar or confusing forms in a test, scrutinize these carefully within the entire context and avoid being misled by features which are conspicuous but which lead to the wrong analogy. For example: Underline any errors that you find in the following sentences and write the correct form above them.

    "John is feeling so behind in his work these days that he certainly isn't interesting in going to the art museum with Kathy." (Note: "interesting" may appear correct by false analogy to "feeling.") etc.

4. Avoid the temptation to choose a form simply because it appears often or is popular. For example: Choose the correct word for the given context in each sentence.

    "Bruce _____ a number of things so rapidly
        a. spoke
        b. said
    that nobody could understand him." etc.

5. Do not assume that there is always a trick to answering an item, but if the item *is* tricky, try to identify all the necessary operations.

6. Deal with all material both in the item stimulus and in the response, guessing where necessary.

7. Use translation sparingly; avoid using it as a crutch.

8. Try thinking in the target language while answering items.

9. Go along with instinct. Do not be too quick to correct items which may be correct to begin with.

Locating the Source of Difficulty in a Test Item or Procedure

Sometimes test items are not very informative because the teacher is not sure where the student's difficulty lies—i.e., at what stage in the processing of the information. In this section, we will consider for purposes of discussion test items requiring a student to *read* some material, precisely because this is an area where feedback is some-times difficult to interpret. For example, if the learner is given a passage to read and then is asked to respond to a series of questions, what is contributing to an incorrect answer? The teacher usually tests for comprehension of a passage by means of questions requiring a fixed, structured, or free response.[2] At times, the teacher is surprised to find that a relatively weak student is able to answer correctly a series of questions about a passage—particularly when the item-response format is multiple-choice—without actually understanding the meaning of the passage overall. More attention to the student's processing of reading passages may help give the teacher a more accurate picture of the student's actual reading level.

We will consider four approaches to assessing errors in reading comprehension at the processing level—i.e., before students provide their "answers" to a test. The four approaches include: (1) miscue analysis of oral reading, (2) ongoing recording of reading strategies, (3) group analysis of multiple-choice distractors, and (4) a contrastive approach to reading grammatical structures.

Miscue analysis of oral reading

Miscue analysis of oral reading consists of the following: The teacher has students read out loud a passage slightly above their reading level. This reading is taped. Students are told at the outset that they will be asked to retell what they have read (to ensure that the student tries to read the passage with comprehension). The teacher plays back the recording and charts errors of omission, substitution, word insertion, and mispronunciation. The analysis also checks for dialect forms, difficulty with word parts, and repetition to correct an error in reading (Allen 1976, Rigg 1976, Buck 1973).

The analysis of the types of miscues is intended to determine whether the student is reading the material with comprehension or not. For example, is a substitution irrelevant or does it significantly change the meaning? In a study of Hebrew-speaking university students' reading of a history text in English, one student read "plane" as "plan," in the sentence, "As a result we live on an economic plane that appears unattainable by them under existing conditions." Asking the student for a Hebrew translation of the sentence indicated that this miscue rendered the sentence meaningless with respect to the rest of the passage and introduced a source of difficulty in interpreting the passage (Cohen and Fine 1978).

As a form of classroom exercise serving as a test for miscues, the teacher can have students take turns reading several sentences out loud. If possible, the teacher jots down all the miscues (or tapes them). The teacher can then have students explain the meaning of what they have just read—either in their native language or in other words in the target language. In this way, the teacher can determine whether the misreading interfered with comprehension of the material and how serious the miscue was. In the above substitution of "plan" for "plane," the miscue obscured the meaning, not just at the sentence level but at the intersentence level as well:

> we enjoy a far more favorable balance between population and natural resources than do they. As a result we live on an economic *plane* that appears unattainable by them under existing conditions. (My italics. E. O. Reischauer and J. K. Fairbank, *East Asia: The Great Tradition*. Boston: Houghton Mifflin, 1960, p. 4)

Clearly, other miscues could be more minor, such as substituting the definite article *the* for the indefinite article *a* in the first sentence above, "we enjoy the far more favorable balance . . ."

The purpose of miscue analysis, as I see it, is to lend a degree of rigor to teacher correction of oral reading. Let us use the example of Hebrew, clearly an extreme case since texts are usually not vowelized, even at beginning levels, and since the alphabet has a series of look-alike letters. Thus students are really engaged in a guessing game when they sight-read aloud (an activity that they are asked to perform rather frequently). During a visit to one advanced class at the university level, I underlined each word that the teacher corrected while the students each read several sentences from a passage. I found that the teacher corrected every fourth word on the average. It is hard to say how much the student readers themselves profited from this rather common approach to correction. As would be expected given this rapid-fire correction approach, the teacher did not distinguish one type of error from another—e.g., an error changing the grammatical function or semantic meaning of the word vs. an error producing a minor phonetic deviation. If the teacher had jotted down the errors and discussed them later, perhaps the exercise of oral reading would have been more enlightening both for the student and for the teacher.

Of course, it is important to note that oral reading is not being endorsed here as a teaching device, but simply as a means for assessing reading problems. It is true, however, that *even* as a test there are problems with oral reading in that, as Knapp (1978) points out, sophisticated reading, for nonnatives as well as for natives, is a "meaning gathering activity" which does *not* involve reading every word. *Oral* reading, however, puts a premium on reading every word, and on reading every word correctly.

Ongoing recording of reading strategies

More and more researchers are trying to determine how reading strategies affect the successful or unsuccessful solution to problems of comprehension. Some research done with adult native readers of English (Aighes et al. 1977) shows that natives only partially understand many words and phrases. They form hypotheses about possible meanings. They reread previous portions, jump ahead, consult outside sources, and make a written record in order to understand what they are reading. Research on the reading strategies of nonnative readers has been conducted by Hosenfeld (1977) in a method similar to the introspective approach that she advocates for investigating strategies that students use to accomplish language exercise (cf. Expected vs. Actual Response Procedure, above).

Hosenfeld developed a system for recording each strategy that the learner uses as he reads—for example, analyzing, translating, attending to grammar, using sentence-level or passage-level context, stopping at an unknown word, skipping an important/inconsequential word or phrase, looking up a word in the back of the book or in a side gloss, viewing the importance of words equally or differently, going back, sounding out a word. She found that out of this introspective, case-study type of analysis, a profile of successful foreign-language readers emerged. Such readers keep the content of the passage in mind as they read, read in broad phrases, skip words viewed as unimportant, skip unknown words and use the remaining words as clues to their meaning, and look up words only as a last resort (Hosenfeld 1977).

In a subsequent study, Hosenfeld (1979) found that a ninth-grade student who had had French since sixth grade and who was in the upper tenth of her class was nonetheless a surprisingly poor reader (as assessed through introspective translation[3] of a relatively simple text). The student was able to perform the typical classroom tasks—reading aloud, contributing to the group, answering textbook questions—without ever having the need to read on her own. Hosenfeld had this reader compare her reading strategies to a protocol for a "contextual guesser" (a successful type of reader according to Hosenfeld's findings). The ninth grader was then asked to list the differences between what she did and what the contextual guesser does (i.e., keeps the story or theme in mind, checks to see if words make sense in context, does not give up). After this "discovery" phase of finding differences in strategies, there was a practical phase in which the student tried out on a new passage strategies that she had not been using. The results showed marked improvement.

It seems reasonable that the use or nonuse of successful reading strategies could influence performance on quizzes and tests involving reading skills. Yet the final grade on the test would not indicate the reading strategies used to obtain that grade. If teachers wish to know more about the reasons for a very high or very low score on a reading exercise, for example, they may find this kind of process-oriented approach quite helpful. It would probably mean special sessions with students during class breaks or after class. Or, as suggested to me by Ruth Berman (personal communication), it could mean following a reading comprehension test with a short probe questionnaire in the native language. For example, sample questions regarding the passage on page 55 could be:

1. When you came to the word "favorable" in the first line, which of the following things did you do?
   a. I knew the word, so I had no trouble.
   b. I translated it into my native language.
   c. I arrived at its meaning from context within the sentence.
   d. I looked up the word in a bilingual dictionary.
   e. I checked to see if the word made sense in the context of the entire passage.
   f. Other. Explain: _____

2. When you read the phrase "as a result" in line 2, what did you do?
   a. I knew that this sentence was connected to the one just preceding it, but didn't know exactly how.
   b. I knew that the second sentence was speaking of the results of what was discussed in the first sentence.

Students could be asked to check off as many strategies as apply to them in their reading of the passage.

Group analysis of multiple-choice distractors

An approach to locating errors in comprehension has been proposed whereby multiple-choice items are designed so that each distractor is intended to attract readers who manifest a particular type of failure to comprehend. These distractors tap failure to understand: (1) the explicit or implicit (inferred) meaning, (2) the conceptual meaning (e.g., quantity, comparison, means, cause), (3) the communicative value of the text (e.g., hypothesis, exemplification, disapproval), (4) the relation between one part of a text and another through cohesive devices (e.g., reference, ellipsis, apposition), or (5) a grammatical relationship between words (Munby 1978b, 1979). This procedure is described in full in Chapter 2. Briefly, the technique calls for students working in small groups to determine what the best answer to a question is, based on a reasoned rejection of the distractors in each question. The actual process of students working on their own and then in groups to find a rationale for eliminating distractors is intended to help the students and the teacher establish whether the students are comprehending correctly or falling prey to one or another type of reading failure.

This type of activity is considered as training for understanding of reading material as opposed to testing for it. The point is that students are to become explicitly aware of what makes one answer right and another answer wrong through this problem-solving approach. A sequel to this activity could then be a more formal testing of reading comprehension through multiple choice, and presumably these students would then be able to perform in a more reasoned way on such a task.

A contrastive approach to reading grammatical structures

Another approach to locating the source of error in reading is through analysis of syntactic patterns found in target-language text material that the learner is reading as contrasted with patterns in similar material in the learner's native language. According to theories describing the effects of first-language interference on second language, learners could be expected to misread a section simply because their expectations about the way the grammar conveys meaning in the target language are conditioned by their experience with grammar in their native language. Thus they would be prone to misinterpret structures that are not just like those in the native language. Cowan (1976) gives examples of such contrastive reading difficulties—for example, native Persian speakers incorrectly processing relative clauses in reading English, and native English speakers incorrectly interpreting co-reference in reading Hindi or word order in reading German.[4] Cowan would suggest that a priori contrastive analysis[5] may lead to correct prediction as to reading difficulties. Teachers do not often verify native-language interference as a source of reading problems, because it calls for extra preparation on the teacher's part, particularly if several language groups are represented in the class.

Ulijn and Kempen (1976) have conducted various types of empirical research to determine the extent to which parallelism of syntactic structures in the target language and first language affect reading in the target language. In several studies, they found that success at reading in the target language (measured in words per second) was not necessarily affected by the presence of target-language syntactic structures different from those in the native language (Ulijn 1977, Ulijn and Kempen 1976). The researchers did, however, identify a condition under which lack of parallelism of syntactic structures in the first language and in the target language could make a difference, namely, when conceptual and referential knowledge is limited. The experimenters hypothesized that under these conditions the readers would be forced to scrutinize the syntactic structure of each sentence and that differences in syntactic patterns between the first language and the target language should hamper comprehension.

A group of Dutch second-year psychology students were asked to read target-language (French) instructions for using an apparatus without actually seeing the apparatus. Then they were told to translate this set of instructions into their native language. Results showed that, in fact, target-language structures created more difficulty in translation when they were not parallel to the Dutch structures. This experiment was intended to demonstrate that subjects will revert to a syntactic reading strategy when they lack conceptual knowledge—in this case, visual cues to inferring the meaning of lexical items. And the researchers claim that once a syntactic reading strategy is employed, there is more likelihood that degree of parallelism of structures between native and target language will play a role.

The importance of the Ulijn and Kempen work is that they have, in fact, addressed themselves empirically to the issue of determining *where* the error or difficulty in reading a second language actually lies. Specifically, they have raised the issue that *if* the learner is employing a syntactic reading strategy, lack of parallelism in structures across languages may interfere with comprehension. A question for the teacher is how to determine when students are employing a syntactic reading strategy.

Instead of asking students to write out a full translation, they could be asked to choose which of two or more sentences in their native language is the best translation of a target-language sentence. The teacher could, for example, have the alternate-choice sentences differ in just one or more syntactic features. But, of course, this approach may draw extra attention to the feature in question and inadvertently simplify the task.

These are just some of the possible means of looking at the processing of material to be tested. We have simply taken examples from reading. We could have turned, for example, to the issue of testing writing and to the process of writing a composition. For example, as Levenston (1978) has recently demonstrated, after a written composition has been corrected for errors (i.e., "reconstructed"), the product still does not usually result in native-like output—either in style or in clarity of thought. Levenston identifies certain influences during the process of writing a composition which result in deviance, and suggests that the clarifying of ambiguities (one step in "reformulating" a composition so that it appears native-like) really involves consulting with the student who wrote the piece. The important point being stressed in this section is that the process that the student uses to perform a task may give as many insights as to the student's abilities in the area being tested as the student's actual right or wrong answer to the questions.

The Effect of Practice on Test Taking

Teachers commonly feel that if students have a chance to practice types of tests and test items over time, their performance on such tests will improve. This belief is conspicuous with regard to examinations such as matriculation examinations. The question is whether such practice is warranted. Research findings with regard to language tests are at best mixed. For example, one study investigated whether 9 weeks of biweekly practice in taking dictation (for listening-comprehension purposes) and in completing cloze passages[6] would produce a greater improvement rate in an experimental group of EFL students than in the control group from pre- to posttesting (Kırn 1972). Eighty-five university students in five classes at three levels of ESL at the University of California, Los Angeles, served as experimental students. Another 114 students served as a control. At each level, half the experimental students were given biweekly practice in taking dictations; the other half were given cloze passages to complete. The practice sessions were not found to produce significantly greater improvement among those receiving the sessions than among the control-group students.

Another study investigated whether there would be a practice effect from repeated administration of a standard EFL test, using different forms (Bowen 1977). Five forms of the Michigan Test of English Language Proficiency were given to 38 students, with 8 days separating each form. It was found that there was no learning from the practice effect of having taken a previous form of the test.

A third study, on the other hand, obtained evidence that learners could enhance their performance on discrete-point items testing phonological, morphological, and syntactic elements of language (Schulz 1977). One group of 35 learners of French at Ohio State University received only tests of simulated communication, and another group of 45 students received only discrete-point tests over 10 weeks of instruction. With respect to the "discrete-point item test," listening comprehension and reading comprehension were assessed through multiple-choice questions (two or more alternatives—written, oral, or recalled from memory); writing and speaking were assessed through structural pattern drills. The "simulated communication test" called for making a spontaneous response (written, oral, or gestural) in a specified realistic situation. Here the emphasis was on meaning, not on linguistic correctness. Sample communication tasks included summarizing in the target language information heard or read in the native language, drawing pictures or following directions on a map according to directions in the target language, and asking and answering questions.

At the end of the time period, the two groups were given both a simulated communication test and a discrete-point item test. Those students who had received the discrete-point treatment performed significantly better on discrete-point items testing listening, reading, and writing, but not speaking in the target language. The students who had received the communication treatment did not, however, perform significantly better on communication tasks. Among other things, the author concluded that discrete-point items take special test-taking skills, the implication being that those who get exposure to such items over time therefore benefit.

It would appear, then, that the research does provide insights into the effect of practice on test taking. If the test is of a more integrated, global, pragmatic nature—as with cloze, dictation, and simulated communication—the effects of practice may be only slight. If the test is of a more discrete-point nature, the learner may well acquire added expertise in handling such items. What this finding may really be saying is that with more pragmatic, "skill-using" measures there is no real need to worry that performance may just be an artifact of the test. Since there is always a fear that the teacher is not getting a true picture of students because some are test-wise and some are not, practice-proof tests may be advantageous. A disturbing thought about Schulz' findings is that they may encourage a teacher to teach to a particular discrete-point test if the teacher knows that success on the test depends on training. Then possibly the test would be dictating the nature of instruction rather than the instructional objectives and course syllabus—a situation that a teacher may wish to avoid.

In Brief

Guidelines exist as to instructions that may accompany a test. In reality, only some of these are adhered to in the writing of a given test. It is useful for a teacher to know what the students actually understand their task to be and how they utilize instructions to perform the required task. It is suggested that a teacher provide a sample item in cases where the format may not be clear, indicate the value of each section (and possibly of each item on a test), and provide suggested time to spend on each section.

Once students are involved in the task itself, the process that they use to complete the task can say a great deal about the product. In an oral interview, the interviewer and respondent work together to compose the social fact referred to as "the answer." On written tests, students may get an item right for the wrong reasons or wrong even though their inferences are well based. The results on paper may not reflect the use or nonuse of reasoning. Students may have sophisticated short cuts for doing exercises, such that they bypass activities that the teacher may have considered an essential part of the task.

Establishing where the breakdown occurs in producing an erroneous answer on a test is not an easy thing to do. Taking the area of reading comprehension, for example, it is possible to gain insights through utilization of techniques such as miscue analysis, recording of the learners' introspective account of their reading strategies, group analysis of multiple-choice distractors, and a contrastive analysis of grammatical structures in the reading material. Such approaches help to provide more information as to why a student arrived at a particular answer.

If language testing is to be a more genuine means for helping the student to learn the language, it would seem that attention should be paid to the process of test taking. In large classes, teachers may have to depend on students' own self-evaluation and insights or on group work, as in student scrutiny of multiple-choice distractors. In smaller classes, it may be possible for teachers to have actual interview sessions in which learners serve as informants as to how they are approaching the task of finding answers to questions.

Notes

1. That is, students mistook the form *metapsim* (present tense prefix *me* + root t-p-s) for a *hitpael* verb like *mitarvim* (present tense prefix *mit* + root a-r-v).

2. A fixed response calls for the respondent to make choices from among existing alternatives (such as with alternate, multiple-choice, or matching-response formats). A structured response allows respondents to contribute some of their own input to the answer (e.g., ordering of elements, identification, or completion). A free response offers respondents the liberty to say or write what they choose, usually within certain parameters.

3. That is, students translate the passage out loud, while providing an ongoing commentary regarding the procedures they are using to perform the translation.

4. Rickard (1979) also found that the reader's first language (Chinese, Japanese, Persian, and Spanish, respectively) influenced perceptual strategies in reading English—specifically, in determining which sentence of a pair was a correct paraphrase or expansion of another sentence.

5. That is, a comparison of forms in the native language and in the target language; see Stockwell, Bowen and Martin (1965) for an example of a contrastive analysis of English and Spanish grammatical structures.

6. See Chapter 5 for more on cloze and dictation tests.

Chapter 4

Preparing a Quiz or Test: A Distinctive - Element Approach

Discrete - Point and Integrative Testing: A Continuum

In recent years, the notion of discrete-point testing, i.e., testing one and only one point at a time. has fallen into some disfavor among theorists. Such an item, for example, testing for verb tense in the auxiliary, follows:

> (Written stimulus) "Did you go to the frisbee tournament last night?"
> (Written multiple-choice completion) "No, I _____ ."
>
> *(a) didn't go
> (b) haven't gone
> (c) hadn't gone

Critics of this approach raise several points of contention. They feel that such a method provides little information on the student's ability to function in actual language-using situations. They also contend that it is difficult to determine *which* points to test. Even if we could assume that a finite list of important points exists, we would still select only a sampling of these points for any given test, and therefore would have to ask whether the items we chose were representative (Spolsky 1968).

Testing points have in the past been determined in part by a contrastive analysis of differences between the language being tested and the native language of the learner. But this contrastive approach in itself has been criticized for being too limiting—too myopic. A rival philosophy of integrative testing emerged, whereby the emphasis was on testing more than one point at a time.

As we will see, there is actually a continuum from the most discrete-point item on the one hand to the most integrative, global items or procedures on the other. Most items fall somewhere in between, regardless of the label attached to them. There is also a distinction to be made between *direct* and *indirect* tests. A direct test samples directly from the behavior being evaluated, while an indirect test is contrived to the extent that the task is different from a normal language-using task (Stolz and Bruck 1976). So there is not only a continuum from the most discrete-point to the most integrative tests but also a dichotomy between direct and indirect tests:

DIRECT TESTING

EXCLUSIVELY
DISCRETE-POINT
(a test comprised of individual discrete-point items tested separately)

INDIRECT TESTING

EXCLUSIVELY
INTEGRATIVE
(a test comprised of items or procedures integrating a number of points)

So, for example, if a student is tested on his ability to give a talk in front of the class and at the same time is tested on usage of specific verb tenses, we say that the test is a "direct" test of a particular behavior—namely, giving a talk, and is concentrating on discrete points, i.e., verb tenses. If the same talk is rated more integratively for a whole range of items, say, in pronunciation, grammar, and lexicon, then we say it is a "direct integrative test." A traditional multiple-choice grammar test with specific items checking for points of grammar could be termed an "indirect discrete-point test" in that it is a contrived situation and one in which the student is not displaying actual grammatical performance, say, in normal classroom routines or even out of class. Finally, an example of an "indirect integrative test" would be a cloze test, which will be discussed in more detail in Chapter 5. This is an indirect test of integrative reading ability in that it is not assessing reading ability directly, but rather the ability to write words into randomly deleted blanks as a measure of reading ability.

There is also a distinction to be made at the more integrative end of the continuum between those tests that are more *pragmatic* in nature and those that are less pragmatic. In effect, pragmatic tests are a subset of integrative tests. What makes a particular integrative test pragmatic is the extent to which students are motivated by the task to really get into the communication act, receptively or productively. Thus, if students throw themselves into a simulated dialog with total abandon, they are providing the teacher with pragmatic test data. Although a test such as a cloze employs an indirect-stimulus format (i.e., measuring reading through *writing* words in blanks), the test would be termed "pragmatic" to the extent that it motivates students to treat the reading passage as a piece of discourse, rather than as a series of individual sentences.

Close scrutiny of items at the more discrete-point end of the continuum reveals that the truly discrete-point item is not easy to construct. A discrete-point item (as in the example above) implies that only one element (e.g., the contracted form of the negative, singular past tense auxiliary: "didn't") from one component of language (e.g., syntax) is being assessed in one skill (reading), which is a receptive (as opposed to "productive") skill. In reality, so-called discrete-point items often test more than one point at a time. For example, if an item calling for a speaker to convert a present tense form into past tense has an oral item stimulus (e.g., the teacher gives the cue, "Did you go to the frisbee tournament last night?"), the item is also testing the skill of listening. Or if the item is testing written syntax, but the respondent must read the item first in order to know what response to write out, the item is also testing reading. For example:

> Read the following sentence, underlining an incorrect form if one exists. Write the correct form at the right margin.
>
> The boys couldn't <u>found</u> their pants   *find*

Such an item has been referred to as a "hybrid" test item in that it is testing several things at the same time (Valette 1977).

Of course, it may be that one or more points required of the students in order for them to answer the question are presumed *not* to cause difficulty and are therefore *not* considered as expicitly among the discrete points being tested. For example, in the written syntax item above, although reading comprehension is a necessary condition for obtaining a correct answer, the teacher may be assuming that all the students will read and understand this stimulus without problems. Good testing practice would, in fact, require that test writers confine source of difficulty *only* to what they want to test. Experience has demonstrated, however, that the test writer's intentions are not always successfully carried out.

For another example of more integrative items, let us turn to items based on discourse analysis of texts. The very systems of meaning that have been identified to describe different layers of meaning in text (Candlin et al. 1978) immediately suggest the almost obligatory integrativeness of attempts to test reading comprehension. These layers of meaning in text include "notional" meaning (basic semantic categories); "propositional" meaning (the information content of the material); "contextual" meaning, consisting of text-level cohesion and discourse-level realization of functional categories like "assertion" and "justification"; and "pragmatic" meaning (referring in this context to the attitude and purpose of the author).

Let us go back to the paragraph appearing in Chapter 2:

> The gap between East and West has also been widened by a growing discrepancy in material standards of living. Nowhere is the contrast sharper than between Americans and the people of Asia. In part because of accidents of history and geography, we enjoy a far more favorable balance between population and natural resources than do they. As a result we live on an economic plane that appears unattainable by them under existing conditions. This economic gap perpetuates and sometimes heightens the difference between our respective attitudes and ways of life. (E. O. Reischauer and J. K. Fairbank. *East Asia: The Great Tradition*. Boston: Houghton Mifflin 1960, p. 6)

Let us assume that this paragraph appeared in a test being read in class and that the teacher had prepared several questions with respect to meaning. For example:

1. According to this paragraph, how similar are Americans and Asians?
2. How are attitudes affected by the economic gap?

Both the above questions could be termed integrative. Each has several specific features that it is testing, and it is testing these in consort. Let us look first at question 1. At the notional level of meaning, the item tests for the lexical item "sharper," which is used in one of its several meanings in place of "clearer," "conspicuous," "noticeable," or something of the kind. Then, the item also tests for comprehension of contextual meaning. At the text level, the reader must perceive that the adjectival phrase "nowhere sharper" provides modifying contrast, and the separation of the two words "nowhere" and "sharper" creates a problem of cohesion. At the level of discoursal meaning, the item checks to see if the reader perceives correctly how the functional category "strength of claim" is realized here—i.e., that when it comes to standard of living, there is *no* greater contrast than between Americans and peoples of Asia. Thus question 1 tests for lexical meaning, textual cohesion, and discoursal meaning.

The second question tests, at the notional level, for lexical meanings. Nontechnical terms like "respective," "perpetuates," and "heightens" may be difficult for nonnatives, as well as technical terms like "economic gap." At the textual level, the question checks for cohesion, specifically for reference, to see if the students realize that "West" = "Americans" = "we," that "East" = "peoples of Asia" = "they," and that the "our" in the third sentence refers to *both* groups. Then, the item also tests for the ability to connect the last sentence with previous sentences, through the determiner "this" in "this economic gap."

Let us now focus primarily on *integrative* testing. The main purpose here is to call attention to those testing techniques that are practical for the language classroom—on short notice, and with a minimum of preparation. They are by no means representative of all possible techniques to test language items. For a comprehensive coverage of language testing items, a number of books are available (e.g., Lado 1961, Valette 1977, Harris 1969, Clark 1972, Heaton 1975). This discussion will consider integrative items on the basis of their component parts—the item-stimulus format, the item-response format, and the tested response behavior. The more traditional means of categorizing items by means of skill—e.g., listening, speaking, reading, and writing—will not be adhered to in this discussion precisely because the *same* or similar stimulus and response formats are often used in testing different skills. Thus the same or similar items seem to keep reappearing as the discussion moves from one skill to the next.

Although models have been developed for the exhaustive analysis of the distinctive elements of language tests (see, for example, Carroll 1968), the purpose here is rather to provide an analysis of just *some* of the elements which can be combined relatively easily to produce a variety of different integrative tests for the classroom. It may be that students function best on tests if they are constantly challenged by a variety of item-stimulus and response formats. Of course, such variety means more teacher effort at test or quiz construction and also requires that students pay closer attention to the items and procedures with which they are dealing.[1]

The next section on test elements is meant to be functional. Describing item types in terms of stimulus and response formats is intended to highlight distinctive elements. Given teachers' awareness of such elements, they can produce not only items which are markedly different but also items which are variations on the same theme. It may help in keeping students alert and in getting a more rounded picture of their ability to vary the *combination* of formats for the item *stimulus* (i.e., oral, written, nonverbal, or a combination) and for the item *response* (likewise oral, written, or nonverbal). Rather than exhaustively providing all possible item-stimulus formats and response formats, only some formats are provided—those which may be usable in class with a minimum of preparation. The section includes the following topics:

Item-stimulus format
  Oral stimulus
    Contextualized minimal pairs
    Sentence with selected grammatical structure
    Conveying of information
    Questions or interview
    Instructions
  Written stimulus
    Sentence stimulus
    Passage stimulus
    Instructions
  Nonverbal stimulus: gestures or pictures
    Type of picture
    Affective value of picture
    Presentation format
    Subject of picture
    Display format
    Purpose of picture
Item-response format
  Oral response
    Oral recitation
    Role playing
    Interviewing
  Oral or written response
    Distinguishing
    Ordering
    Combination
    Identification
    Completion
    Paraphrase
    Structured or free response
  Written reporting response
    Matching
    Note taking
    Rewriting
  Nonverbal response
    Gestures
      Identification
      Responding to requests
    Pictorial response

The discussion then moves to consideration of the tested response behavior—quantity, accuracy, and speed.

What this discussion does not do is give a cookbook listing of items by skill area (listening, speaking, reading, and writing). Taking the stimulus and response features and generating items is left up to the teacher using this book. The approach here is of providing a "grab bag" of features to combine into a given test.

So, let us say that the teacher wants to test for knowledge of the simple past tense in English. Then the teacher might choose a written stimulus, such as a sentence (page 72), and a written response, such as "rewriting" (page 81), i.e., transforming the verb in the sentence into past tense. Or a teacher who wants to have a quick group measure of conversational ability but does not have time to assess each student's speaking ability could choose as an item-stimulus format an oral set of instructions (page 72) as to how to play a particular character in a play. For expediency, the item-response format could be written. In other words, students would be requested to write out a script (page 82) reflecting as much as possible the way that the character would say the lines if it were acted out orally.

Item-Stimulus Format

The teacher has the option to use one of three different formats for eliciting language behavior: oral, written, and nonverbal (through gestures or pictures). He can also use some combination of these to assess language. Let us look at these in turn.

Oral stimulus

The use of an oral stimulus could imply a variety of formats. To start with, is the oral stimulus the teacher's voice or that of one or more others? For example, the voice could be that of students, perhaps at varying levels of target-language proficiency. It could be the voice of a commentator or other professional. Is the voice live—in person or from a telephone—or recorded on audio or videotape? Is the input clear or distorted—i.e., is there noise (perhaps purposely) in the background? Is the input natural speech, oral reading of material as if natural speech, or oral reading of material as formal oral recitation? Is the pace fast or slow, natural or unnatural? Some recorded oral dialogs, for example, sound funny to native speakers because they immediately perceive that a native would never say it that way—with stilted, drawn-out pronunciation, at an unusually slow speed.

The following are some suggested oral formats for item stimuli to be used in the classroom.

Contextualized minimal pairs.   A teacher or a student says (reads) a sentence containing a target-language sound. The sound is contextualized in a sentence. The speaker then gives the sentence again, either substituting a word containing a sound which is a minimal pair for the target sound or leaving the original word as it was (Lado 1961, chapter 7; Brière 1967; Bowen 1972). For example:

1. He's *heating* the fish.
2. He's *hitting* the fish.

With respect to teaching EFL, books exist which provide vowel and consonant contrasts in initial, medial, and final position, and which provide contextualized minimal pairs such as in the above example. Nilsen and Nilsen (1971) provide minimal pairs in English based on phonemic discrimination problems of learners from 50 different language backgrounds. Since the format is simply one of contextualized minimal pairs delivered orally, the content could also involve testing for awareness of, say, grammatical markers. For example:

1. He *hits* the ball.
2. He *hit* the ball.

Here again the speaker either gives sentence 1 twice, sentence 2 twice, or 1 and 2 in either order. (Both for this example and for the previous one, the *response* format could be, say, nonverbal identification or oral distinguishing.)

Sentence with selected grammatical structure.   Sentences containing tense, number, gender, a combination of these, or other elements of interest are read aloud. For example:

A boy's making the mess.
(Singular subject + contracted copula + present progressive + definite article + object.)

We note that even such a short sentence has a number of testable grammatical features. For example, despite the definite article *a,* students may interpret *boy's* as the plural *boys.* (One possible *response* format would be oral or written identification—e.g., singular or plural.) The item could also be testing for ability to distinguish the contacted auxiliary forms of *is* and *has*—e.g., "a boy is"/"a boy has." (Then a *response* format might be oral or written distinguishing—a boy has/a boy is/ a boy's (possessive).)

Conveying of information.   Students hear an informant talk, lecture, or discuss, in person or through the media. They are then asked questions orally to test comprehension of content or form. The information can also be in written form so that students can follow along while they listen. If a simulated lecture is used, the teacher should see that it has the normal false starts, repetitions, filled pauses,[2] and the like, that give it normal qualities of redundancy. If a "lecture" is actually simply the reading of a printed text, it is really testing for, say, the comprehension of text read orally—not of a lecture.

Questions or interview.   Students are asked questions individually (e.g., to spot-check a grammar point (Chastain 1976, p. 506)). For example, the question is posed and then a student is named. The teacher might even select the student randomly from a set of name cards to introduce the element of chance. Once students' names have been drawn, their cards may be set aside so that they are not called again until the next activity, or perhaps their name cards are kept in the pack to keep them alert. For example:

> Teacher: "What happened to Harvey after he slipped on the banana peel?"
> "Carlos?"

The teacher may also ask a series of questions in the form of an interview and have this constitute all or part of a test. For example:

> Teacher: What do you think actually happened in that terrorist attack?
> Teacher: Do you think the authorities handled it well?
> Teacher: What is the likelihood of similar attacks in the future?

Instructions.   A student is given instructions to interview someone else. For example:

> You are the host on an evening talk show and are now interviewing a man who teaches parrots, parakeets, and other birds how to talk. It is your task to ask a series of stimulating questions.

Students could also be given a situation and be asked to react, or more indirectly, could be asked to say what they would say in that particular situation (Levenston 1975). For example:

> Your neighbor's dog was on the porch barking at the crack of dawn for the third day in a row. This time you're fed up. You go next door to complain.
> Neighbor (opening door with a big smile on his face and shakes his neighbor's hand): "Come in pal."
> Student: (The student role plays and responds directly.)
>
> or
>
> Student (indirect approach): "If my neighbor's dog woke me up three days in a row and I were going next door to complain, I would . . ."

Or students could be given secret instructions as to how to play a particular role in a role-playing situation (Valette 1977, p. 155). For example:

> One student is told in secret that he is to play the role of a plainclothes policeman and he has just encountered the student activist responsible for starting a violent riot on campus last week. Another student is told that he is to play the role of a withdrawn, serious student with no interest in politics. He is told that a student prankster is running around, impersonating a plainclothes policeman.

For a final suggestion, students are asked to describe the events they are witnessing. What they witness could be acted out live—i.e., a dramatization in class. It could also be on videotape or on film. For example:

> A student comes into the room, pretending to be a robber. He is holding a banana in his hand as if it were a revolver. The teacher, in fright, hands over her money. The student exits rapidly with the money, eating the banana and dropping the peel in the wastepaper basket on his way out of the room.

The above types of instructions could also be written, so that the students can follow along at the same time that they hear the instructions given orally.

Written stimulus

Sentence stimulus. The student is given fragments of a sentence out of order and must arrange them in the proper order. For example:

I had seen	immediately reminded me	Albert's face
A	B	C

in a zoo	of a silly monkey
D	E

Correct order: <u>C</u>   <u>B</u>   <u>E</u>   <u>A</u>   <u>D</u>

The student reads a sentence and is asked to perform a variety of functions—e.g., correct it grammatically; transform it to another person, tense, or number; or paraphrase it. For example:

Correct the grammar:
 "I have counselors which already finish the army."
Paraphrase the following sentence so that it reflects the way a native speaker would say it:
 "I have counselors who already finished the army."—surface corrections.
 "The counselors working here have already finished their army duty."—The way a native would probably say it.

The student is given a sentence with a word or phrase missing, possibly preceded by a sentence or two to set the context. The student is to fill in the word. For·example:

> Nobody seemed to know what had happened to Herbert's portable TV. He had set it down on the bench while he was playing basketball. He had no choice but to _____ the loss to the police.

Students are given two separate sentences that they are to combine into one. For example:

> That lemon meringue pie is hard to resist.
> I am on a strict diet.

Passage stimulus.   The student is given a passage to read and then is asked to write answers to questions. These questions could be posed explicitly (e.g., a direct question about a structure) or implicitly (e.g., a general-comprehension question involving the structure). Categories of questions could tap different levels of meaning: semantic categories, the informational content of the passage, textual cohesion, the discoursal functions of the material (e.g., classification, definition), and the author's attitude (Candlin et al. 1978). It might be that the students themselves are responsible for writing their own questions to go with a given passage. These would serve as a stimulus if the students then answered them. If the writing of the questions were an end in itself or part of the "response" that the passage was the stimulus for, this activity would fall under oral or written response (below), specifically structural or free response.

Instructions.   The student is given written instructions to write a certain type of composition, e.g., a narrative, a descriptive piece, or a comparative composition:

> Write a narrative discussing what you did last summer and what you intend to do this summer.
>
> Describe what you consider to be the basic requirements for a happy life.
>
> Compare the character of the people and pace of life in two major cities with which you are familiar.

Perhaps teachers may intend for the narrative to elicit past and future tenses, the "happy life" essay to elicit nouns, and the comparison of people in two cities to elicit adjectives. If so, they may wish to stipulate that students use a certain number of words from the given form class and particular verb tenses, to ensure that such forms appear in the students' essays. It has been demonstrated that assigning a particular topic does not automatically control the frequency of parts of speech (Brière 1964).

Nonverbal stimulus: gestures or pictures

Gestures can serve as the item-stimulus format, especially if knowledge of culture-specific nonverbal behavior is being tested. In other words, the teacher makes a given gesture and then this is coupled with some item-response format (see below) by which the students indicate a knowledge or lack of knowledge of the particular gesture. Numerous sources can be found regarding varieties of nonverbal behavior within and across language groups (see, for example, Key 1977, pp. 136–138).

A more frequently used nonverbal stimulus is a picture. In fact, it could even be a picture of a gesture. However, a number of reservations can be made about using pictorial stimuli. For example, preparing pictures takes teacher time. Finding ready-made pictures also takes time. Pictures may be interpreted in various ways, either because they are simply ambiguous (Valette 1977, p. 223) or because they presuppose a certain cultural background, educational level, socioeconomic status, or age (Harris 1969; Heaton 1975, pp. 74–75). In light of the difficulties in interpreting complex pictures, Clark (1972, p. 52) recommends that pictures used in tests be simple, stylized, and free of distracting background or superficial detail.

Despite the various reservations, well-designed pictures can serve useful functions. They can get stimulus information across to the students without the use of elaborate verbiage. In fact, pictures may be crucial if teachers do not want a supposed measure of their students' ability to write a composition to be actually a test of their ability to, say, read and correctly interpret a set of instructions about what to write on. Furthermore, a pictorial stimulus format helps eliminate the problem of students' simply lifting verbatim from a verbal stimulus material to use in the response (Heaton 1975, p. 133). It has also been pointed out that pictures can be used to elicit conversation between a tester and a respondent (Heaton 1975, p. 90). Commercial tests of oral language, in fact, rely heavily on pictures to elicit data.

The Ilyin Oral Interview (Ilyin 1976), intended to assess English as a second language for upper elementary through adult learners, consists of two parallel sets of pictures with accompanying questions. The pictures illustrate in black and white a series of actions during a day in the past (e.g., yesterday), today, and during a day in the future (e.g., tomorrow). There is a picture of a clock next to each drawing, indicating the time that the activity took place during the day. The Bilingual Syntax Measure (Burt, Dulay, and Hernández-Chavez 1975) contains seven humorous cartoon drawings in color, the last three being in a story sequence.

In actual fact, pictures do not usually appear alone as a stimulus for language items (as they might in a nonverbal subtest of intelligence, e.g., "analogy" or "classification" subtest), but rather in conjunction with some oral or written material. The item-stimulus format, then, consists of, say, a written passage, accompanied by four pictures, only one of which depicts what is described in the passage.

An appraisal both of commercially available formats and of the pictorial stimuli serving as examples in various books on language testing yielded the following breakdown into relevant dimensions: type of picture, affective value of picture, presentation format, subject of picture, display format, and purpose of picture. We will deal with each of these in turn.

Type of picture.   A picture may be a simple sketch, e.g., stick figures; it may be a complete drawing; or it may even be a painting with full detail (as used in the Dailey Language Facility Test (Dailey 1968, Silverman et al. 1976)). It may also be a photograph (Figure 1). As mentioned above, reservations have been raised concerning detailed

Figure 1   Different types of pictures

pictures. Perhaps the extent of detail depends on the population. When the Dailey test of oral language, employing a photograph, a painting, and a sketch, was used with young bilingual children (K–3) in the Redwood City study (Cohen 1975c), it appeared that in both languages the children most enjoyed describing the sketch. Perhaps it was because this format allowed them the most room for imagination in their stories.

Affective value of picture. The picture can be intended as serious or humorous. Sometimes the element of humor is introduced by cartoons, particularly through the use of exaggerated or imaginary elements. Since humor is situationally based, it is possible to be humorous even with stick figures (see Figure 2).

Figure 2 Depicting a Picnic Humorously

Presentation format. Pictures can be used individually, in a group, or in a series. There is an important difference between a group and a series. In a group, two or more pictures may be the same except for one feature, and the student must choose which picture is being referred to (see Figure 3). Or the pictures in the group may be quite different from one another, and only a proper understanding of some oral or written input will lead the student to the correct choice (see Figure 4).

In a series of pictures, there is a chronology from one picture to the next (see Figure 5).

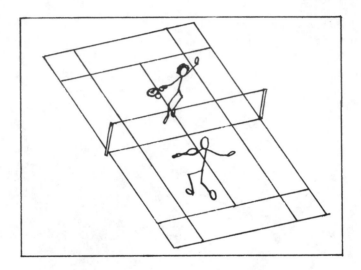

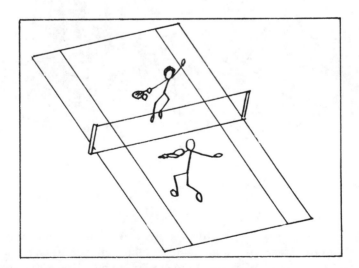

Figure 3   Locating the missing feature: a tennis match

Figure 4   Identifying the mentioned tree swing

Figure 5   Depicting a story about a baby

Subject of picture.   The picture may be that of some object or person(s). The object may be illustrated so as to stress size, shape or color specifically. With both people and objects, the picture may be intended to elicit some action, e.g., an action verb like "pushing" (see Figure 6).

Part of the criticism of certain traditional pictorial tests is that they focused too much on objects and too little on people engaged in pictorially interesting events (Oller 1979).

Figure 6   Depicting action verbs: *push!*

Display format.   For test purposes, students must be able to see the pictures. One approach is through the preparation of transparencies to be used with an overhead projector. Perhaps filmstrips could provide another medium for conveying the test stimulus. The teacher may even be able to display one picture in front of the class (e.g., a picture from a magazine pasted on a board) if all the students can view it well enough. Teachers may also copy the picture onto a ditto, but this calls for more skill and preparation time on the part of the teacher, and unintentional imprecision may make the picture(s) difficult for students to interpret.

Purpose of picture.   Pictures can serve a variety of functions. For example, two or more pictures may be used to stimulate comparison across pictures, in search of the correct answer. A picture may elicit a narrative or discussion, or it may be used to check for written or oral comprehension of a series of statements. The student is to indicate whether on the basis of the picture the statements are true or false. A picture can also be meant to recreate a situation under discussion. For example, a picture can represent a dangerous intersection where accidents often happen. The student is to describe the intersection and mention some of the accidents and their causes (Heaton 1975, p. 133).

Item-Response Format

Teachers can have students respond to test items in one of three ways—orally, in writing, or nonverbally (through gestures or pictures).

Oral response

Oral recitation.   After students have had a chance to read a passage silently, they are asked to read it aloud. They can read aloud in several ways, depending on the material. The material can be written to be read as if spoken (e.g., lines from a play), to be read in an informational style (e.g., news broadcast), or to be read as recitation (adapted from Gregory 1967).

Role playing.   Students participate in impromptu role playing in which they are acting upon secret instructions.[3]

Interviewing.   Students are given information (possibly in the native language) that they are to obtain by interviewing someone else in the target language.

Oral or written response

Distinguishing.   Students indicate that an item is true/false, correct/incorrect, one or two, yes/no, same/different—orally or in writing; or students select the correct answer from, say, four multiple choices.

Ordering.   Students arrange fragments of a sentence, a set of paragraphs, and so forth, in their proper order.

Combination.   The student combines two sentences into a single complex one.

Identification.   Students indicate whether an utterance refers to past, present, or future tense by supplying "yesterday," "today," or "tomorrow" after hearing an utterance or reading some material which employs one of the three tenses. In like manner, students can indicate whether a verb is in a singular or plural form by supplying pronouns such as "he," "she," or "they"; or the students could simply mark an X next to the appropriate picture:

(Valette 1977, pp. 101–102).

Completion.   Students supply a word or phrase (e.g., a phrasal verb) missing from a sentence or passage.

Paraphrase.   Students produce another sentence or set of sentences that has the same information as contained in the stimulus sentence or sentences, but without using the same content words (except proper nouns). For example:

> Stimulus: Penelope construed from Dudley's remarks that he was intent on accomplishing his goal.
>
> Student response: Penelope took Dudley's comments to mean that he was set on achieving his aim.

In this example, the surface structure of the paraphrase is similar to that of the original sentence. A paraphrase could also call for some transformation, such as from active to passive voice. But then the teacher should be mindful that the transformed sentence may be only a partial paraphrase. For example:

> John took Mary home.   ≠   It was John that took Mary home.

Actually, tight or rigorous paraphrase is in some ways a special skill— one that natives may not necessarily be good at. But rough paraphrasing is something that second-language learners do quite frequently as a strategy for getting around material they do not know well (see Tarone, Cohen, and Dumas 1976).

Structured or free response.   Students answer questions about a news broadcast, a lecture, a casual talk, or a passage in their native language or in the second language. Whereas in many situations it is taken for granted and even obvious that students are to write answers in the second language, under certain circumstances it may be more effective to have the students respond in their native language (see Nation 1978, TESOL 1978). Laufer (1978), for example, reporting on an experiment that she conducted among university-level English-as-a-foreign-language students in Israel, notes that in a context where the course emphasis is on comprehension of specialized texts and where writing is not taught as a skill, there are problems in having students write open-ended answers in the second language (in this case, English) and advantages to having them write such answers in the native language (in this case, Hebrew). Her research findings suggest that native-language answers may be preferable as an indicator of reading comprehension (given the nature of the course and the student population).

In other words, it is important to consider how students use the second language for performing functional tasks outside the language classroom. Supposing that when students read a textbook in a foreign language, they take notes in the native language, use a bilingual dictionary, and translate excerpts for use in term papers and exams in the second language. Furthermore, when they listen to a lecture in a foreign language, they also take notes in their native language, translate sentences into the native language for use in papers and exams, and even ask questions in their native language. In such instances, testing exercises which elicit student responses in their native language would appear not only natural but preferable. The real question would be: How effectively are students translating foreign-language material into their native language? Assuming this translation goes on anyway, it may be valuable to check how accurate it is.

The problems with target-language answers include uncertainty as to whether the answer was simply copied from the text (sometimes with irrelevant material included); the difficulties in deciphering ambiguous or incomprehensible answers due to grammatical or vocabulary problems, punctuation, etc.; and the real possibility of teacher distraction from the *content* of the answers because of the *form*—negatively affecting teachers' judgments about the information. Of course, there are problems with responses in the native language as well. The teachers have to be familiar enough with the students' first language so that they can evaluate whether answers are correct. Furthermore, the students have to be able to find native-language equivalents for the vocabulary and grammatical patterns of the text with which they are working.[4]

Reporting.   Students describe events that they have witnessed.

Written response

Matching.   The student locates a match for a word or phrase, i.e., a word or phrase that is a contextual paraphrase (a synonymous phrase) for another phrase in the given context. For example:

> Read the following paragraph and write out the contextual paraphrase for each of the underlined phrases appearing elsewhere in the text:
>
> On the day before the voting took place, the politicians were still making the kind of outlandish assertions with which they had started their campaigns. The amazing thing was that many of the voters were wont to believe every word that they heard. Yet anyone in his right mind should have been able to identify the type of preposterous statements being issued as just so much politicking before the ballots were cast.
>
> Answers: the kind of outlandish assertions = the type of preposterous statements
>
> ballots were cast = voting took place

Note taking.   A student takes notes on a lecture, news broadcast, or talk. These notes themselves may constitute the response, or the student may then be asked to summarize what was said, or to provide structured or free responses to questions.

Rewriting.   A student is to rewrite a passage, changing one or more elements, e.g., from present to past tense, from first person to third person, from singular to plural, from direct speech to indirect speech.

Nonverbal Response

Gestures

Identification

Classmates can be requested to hold up one finger if they hear the teacher or a fellow student say, "They *hit* the bottle," and two fingers if they hear, "They *heat* the bottle."

Responding to requests

Students can be asked to respond to imperatives—e.g., "Put your hands on your head after you've touched your toes." Or a student could be asked to find a place on a map from a description, arrange blocks or other items according to a description, or identify one of several pictures from a description.

Pictorial response

Like pictorial-stimulus formats, pictorial-response formats are problematic. In a response format, students are being called on to demonstrate some artistic ability—even if it is simply to draw an arrow between two objects or complete some stick drawing. Also, such a format may encourage students to check what other students are doing, which may constitute cheating if this activity is not what the teacher had intended. All the same, partial and total drawing can constitute a change of pace and may be enjoyable for the students.

If the students are asked to draw, the possibilities are somewhat limited. The most reasonable type of picture to request would be stick figures or a simple sketch. Heaton (1975, pp. 73–74) suggests having students draw geometric shapes in various places on the page or, given a street scene, for example, having them supply a number of missing elements, provided orally or in a written list. Figure 7 presents an example in following instructions, aimed specifically at checking for comprehension of vocabulary frequently used with reference to homework assignments—e.g., "to circle," "to underline," "to box in," "to add," "to delete," and "to substitute." Figure 8 involves

Following Directions

You are to read this material carefully and to perform the following tasks:

1. Draw a circle around every letter *t* appearing in this exercise. ↓

2. Underline any word with a double letter in it. ↓

3. Box in this one instruction. ↓

4. Add an arrow pointing downward at the end of every numbered instruction. ✗ *

5. Delete the arrow added to the previous instruction and substitute an asterisk in its place. ↓

Figure 7

completing a picture. Needless to say, the picture-completion exercise is meaningful only insofar as it assesses objects that have been taught in the course. For example, suppose there has been extensive work on prepositional relationships. Picture completion would check for this.

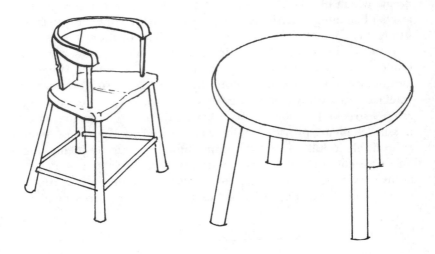

1. Draw a boy sitting beside the chair.
2. Draw two pencils above the table.
3. Draw a tennis ball between the table and the chair.
4. Draw a piece of paper under a leg of the table.

Figure 8   Completing the picture

Tested Response Behavior

Similar items or procedures can be used to test different response behavior. For example, students who are asked to write *accurately* for 20 minutes about their best friend and are told to pay attention to grammar and mechanics will approach the task differently from students who are told to write as much as they can about their best friend in 10 minutes with the emphasis on *speed* and *quantity* of information. Without question, the two tasks will produce different results. In the same way, a reader may be given an hour to read accurately five pages of an article on energy conservation in order to answer ten questions calling for detailed responses. Or the reader may be asked to read rapidly a few selected paragraphs from the article in order to indicate the main idea of each paragraph.

A student can be asked to listen closely to a reporter's question and a dignitary's answer at a press conference, so that the student is tested for *accuracy* of comprehension of the question and of the answer, or to listen to the entire press conference in order to identify the major points that came up.

Thus different response behaviors can be tested with the same material: quantity, accuracy, or speed. Pragmatic testing would place less emphasis on accuracy at the level of grammar and mechanics and more on handling of a greater quantity of material at a native-like rate of speed. When learners are tested for accuracy, they may (1) listen so intently to a part of the message that they miss the message in its entirety, (2) speak with repeated pauses, or (3) read with numerous regressions. The constraint of timing a test or quiz may help to give the student added confidence to function pragmatically in the new language. Practical suggestions have been provided, for instance, regarding a speedwriting task in class, whereby a topic is introduced and written on the blackboard. Then the teacher leads a short guided discussion about the topic, writing key points on the board in an organized fashion. Students then write for seven minutes about some aspect of the topic that is of particular concern to them, at the end of which time the papers are collected (Celce-Murcia 1974).

Wrap-up

This chapter has suggested that instead of talking about discrete-point items and integrative items separately, we give more focus to items and procedures that are somewhere along a continuum from most discrete-point to most integrative. Such an approach encourages the teacher to pay attention to all the things that a particular item tests for. Furthermore, we would note whether this test, which was somewhere along the continuum from discrete-point to integrative, was measuring the actual behavior *directly* (e.g., testing discrete points of grammar in an actual student speech in the classroom) or was measuring the behavior *indirectly* (e.g., testing integrative reading through a cloze test). Also, if the test was more integrative in nature, we would note how pragmatic it was—i.e., the extent to which it motivated students to display their functional ability in the second language.

The chapter then provides a distinctive-element analysis of item-stimulus and item-response formats that might be combined successfully for the purposes of classroom testing—often involving no more than short quizzes. The breakdown of items by skill—listening, speaking, reading, and writing—is purposely avoided since formats cut across skill boundaries and since such breakdowns are found in a number of books on language testing. The approach taken here has rather been that of demonstrating to the teacher the advantage of scrutinizing the truly distinctive elements of test construction. In other words, with a few elements the teacher may construct a variety of classroom quizzes or tests.

Another dimension related to testing formats, namely, the tested response behavior, is also looked at, in that the job of testing does not end once items have been selected. It is important to determine the type of response behavior desired, in terms of speed, accuracy, and quantity.

While this chapter has looked at a range of items on the continuum from discrete-point testing to totally integrative testing, the next chapter looks at just several of the tests on the integrative side, specifically those that are considered more pragmatic in nature.

Notes

1.   There is some evidence with young children (third grade), for example, that tests with *multiple* item formats (in this case, 16 formats on a criterion-referenced test) may produce *poorer* results than tests using a single format (in a standardized test), particularly among children with limited cognitive flexibility and short attention spans (Rodríguez-Brown and Cohen 1979).

2.   Noises like *uh* or *er* which indicate that speakers are continuing but have stopped to choose what they will say next.

3.   An adventuresome teacher may even be willing to have the students engage in "real play"—i.e., role play out of class in the actual setting with a native speaker of the target language playing one major role (e.g., car dealer, furniture store manager, etc.) (Jenks 1979).

4.   See TESOL (1978) for a list of arguments against translating in a foreign-language class, primarily where the emphasis is on learning the oral-aural skills and on writing—not just on reading.

Chapter 5

Assessing Functional Language Ability: A Focus on Three Integrative Tests

There are actually two ways of assessing "functional language ability" (also referred to as "skill using" and "pragmatic ability"). As noted in Chapter 4, we can *directly* assess the behavior that we are interested in or we can assess it *indirectly* through a task different from a normal language-using task. Thus, for example, cloze and dictation tests (to be discussed below) do not reflect actual tasks that a learner of a second language would have to indulge in at work, although they are meant to tap behaviors called for in such situations. On the other hand, a simulated invitation over the telephone could constitute a functional situation akin to what the learner would encounter outside of class.

Whereas Jones (1977) feels that cloze and dictation are only means of evaluating linguistic knowledge, and not functional language ability, Oller (1979) views such tests as requiring both linguistic ability and the ability to relate the sequences of linguistic elements to their normal appropriate pragmatic context. This chapter will explore the position that Oller espouses. We will take cloze, dictation, and a dialog as a point of departure for discussing the testing of functional language ability.

It is interesting that the pendulum may be swinging back away from the testing of functional language ability toward a closer reassessment of how to test linguistic ability, specifically language proficiency. For example, there appears to be renewed interest in the testing of "implicit linguistic knowledge," now concentrating on psychological components or a set of "capacities" which can be tested— such as word-frequency estimation, second-langue memory span, and second-language spew[1] (Upshur 1978). This redirection suggests that the popularity of integrative testing may ultimately wane, and that any one integrative test, such as cloze, is destined not to be the ultimate answer. It is important to state this reservation so that the reader realizes that the following tests are discussed not because they provide an ultimate answer but because they are highly representative of a current wave in integrative testing—a wave which may be out of fashion in the years to come.

We will look first at cloze and dictation, as two indirect integrative tests, using a written response format, and then at a direct integrative test, a staged dialog, using a spoken response format.

Cloze

The "cloze" test has no doubt become one of the most talked about tests of the 1970s (Jones 1977). Although the elicitation of completion or "closure" of blanks deleted from a text evolved in the 1950s in reference to determining the readability of passages in the reader's native language (Taylor 1953), the technique was soon applied to the measurement of reading comprehension in first language and then to achievement in second-language reading as well. However, because early research results were not positive, the cloze test did not rise quickly in popularity. Carroll, Carton, and Wilds (1959), for example, found their cloze instruments to be unreliable and questioned the validity of such a test in measuring foreign-language proficiency. In a follow-up summary of several subsequent research efforts, Carroll (1972) suggested that the ability to supply missing elements in a passage calls for a special ability to use redundancy in a passage—an ability which is independent of verbal ability. He emphasized that the basis of cloze was in fact working with the "local redundancy" of a passage—i.e., that the linguistic cues in the immediate environment (generally in the same sentence) of a missing word tended to supply it. Carroll concluded that the cloze was too crude an instrument to permit one to measure the degree to which an individual comprehends particular lexical or grammatical cues or possesses knowledge of specific language rules. Of course, what Carroll might view as a "crude" measure of degree of comprehension, other researchers may view as an integrative, global measure.

Other findings have been mostly positive. Researchers like Darnell (1968) and Oller (1973, for example) concluded from their studies that it was valuable to the field of testing to popularize the use of cloze and to pursue a course of research regarding cloze. Subsequently, Oller and others (Oller 1974; Chihara, Oller, Weaver, and Chávez-Oller 1977) have attempted to demonstrate that ability to fill in cloze items is not just a matter of perceiving local redundancy but rather involves an awareness of the flow of discourse across sentences and paragraphs. Alderson (1978), on the other hand, did *not* find performance on the cloze as a whole to be based on awareness of the larger context. He suggests that only a small subset of items on a cloze with deletion (discussed below) will tap the reader's ability to comprehend text rather than just isolated phrases (Charles Alderson, personal communication). Researchers are now turning to closer scrutiny of what each cloze blank actually tests (e.g., Nir and Blum-Kulka, forthcoming), and we hope such procedures will help us better interpret statistical findings such as those of Alderson.

Now let us speak to the following issues: what the cloze test is, what it can be used to do, what it is measuring, and what is involved in scoring and assessing cloze results.

What the basic cloze consists of

A cloze test in its basic form is a passage from which after every certain number of words, a word is deleted according to a fixed-ratio procedure. In other words, after, say, one sentence of unbroken text, a word somewhere in the second sentence is deleted and then every nth word thereafter is also deleted (this is often every 5th, 6th, or 7th word). The following is an example of deletion of every 6th word:

People today are quite astounded by the rapid

improvements in medicine. Doctors _____	1.	are
1		
becoming more specialized and _____ drugs	2.	new
2		
are appearing on the _____ daily. At the same	3.	market
3		
time, _____ are dismayed by the inaccessi-	4.	people
4		

bility _____ doctors when they are	5.	of
5		
needed. _____ doctors' fees are constantly on	6.	Whereas
6		
_____ rise, the quality of medical	7.	the
7		
_____ has reached an abysmal low.	8.	care
8		

There has been a general attitude, on the basis of intuition and some research (e.g., Oller 1973), that the cloze is easier the more words there are between deletions because increased context improves comprehension. A recent study, however, found that a cloze test based on the deletion of every sixth word was not more difficult than one based on the deletion of every twelfth word (Alderson 1978).

The *passage* to be selected may either be of particular relevance to the students being tested—e.g., a history passage for students in the humanities—or it may be a passage of general interest. Research has demonstrated that familiarity with the subject matter will improve performance (see, for example, Moy 1975). Furthermore, it has been suggested that if the cloze is to be used as a projective measure of speaking ability (see below), the passage should consist of a transcription of actual spontaneous conversation and not be based on a written text (Hughes 1978).

The research literature has tended to recommend that a cloze have 50 deletions, and thus a minimum length of 250 words in the passage (i.e., using fifth-word deletion). To test this recommendation empirically, an item-analysis program which artificially lengthens cloze tests (using seventh-word deletion) one item at a time was designed (Rand 1978). The program provided standard statistics for a two-item, three-item, four-item, and so forth, up to a fifty-item cloze test for four different scoring methods (exact-word, acceptable-word, clozentropy,[2] and multiple-choice). By twenty-five items, the maximum reliability had been achieved across scoring methods. The conclusion was that little precision is gained by making a cloze test longer than 25 items.

It has also been pointed out that sometimes discretionary judgment must be used when applying the fixed-ratio approach (Oller 1979). For example, if the word which is supposed to be deleted is a proper noun or a low-frequency word lacking common synonyms or a word that would invite too many replacement words, the test constructor may wish to delete an adjacent word instead. Of course, a low-frequency word may be deleted if this word appears elsewhere in the text, since part of reading skill is recognizing lexical repetition. Furthermore, if a word is a "key" word, without which the passage is less comprehensible, or if the word most probably is a new word to students, or part of an unfamiliar idiom, deleting an adjacent word is recommended. It may also be advisable to avoid deleting part of an idiom, particularly if the idiom is not a common one. Whereas deletion of the same word several times is perfectly acceptable, excessive deletion of function words like "and" and "the" should be avoided.

It is valuable to try out a cloze test on a native speaker because other problems may also crop up. For example, the text itself may have one or more awkward sentences with, say, unusual collocations of words. If so, deletion of one may make the correct completion difficult even for natives. In such cases, the sentence itself should be edited to read more naturally. For example, as I was reviewing an English-language cloze, I found myself unable to restore words to the first two blanks in a sentence having five blanks:

From the beginning of the 19th century, _____	when
the slave system began _____ geographic and	its
demographic explosion, the vast _____ of the	majority
Southern slaves _____ Creoles—i.e., born as	were
slaves in the New _____ _____ . . .	World

The correct restoration of the second phrase of the sentence, "*when the slave system began its* geographic and demographic explosion" did not meet my expectations about acceptable collocations in English. I was perplexed by what seemed like an awkward phrase semantically—namely, that "a slave system begins an explosion." Another native reviewer of the test was also unable to supply "when," and supplied "a" instead of "its." In cases like these, it may pay to edit the original phrase itself and then to delete words from it—e.g., "when the slave system began to expand both geographically and demographically" ("When _____ slave system began to expand _____ geographically and demographically, the vast _____ of . . .").

For all the discretionary modifications on a purely random deletion, the basic cloze still does not, however, reflect systematic deletion of purposively selected items—such as prepositions, articles, nouns, verbs, and so forth. This is because the cloze test as a pragmatic test is intended to tap global skills in an integrative fashion (Aitken 1977, Oller 1979). Deliberate deletion of, say, grammar points such as verbs for tense or number makes it more a discrete-point test.

The basic cloze has been tried out in English on learners of English studying in English-mother-tongue countries (Oller 1973) and on learners of English in non-English-mother-tongue countries (Stubbs and Tucker 1974, Moy 1975, Anderson 1976, Cooper and Fishman 1977). Cloze tests have also appeared in other languages, including Amharic, Thai, Vietnamese, German, Japanese, Russian, Spanish, French, and Hebrew (see, for example, Bowen 1969, Oller et al. 1972, Brière et al. 1978, Hanzeli 1979, Nir and Cohen, in press). Cloze tests have also been tried out successfully on younger learners of second languages at school (grades 4 and 5) to determine the minimal age and language-exposure requirements in order for the test to be reliable and valid (Lapkin and Swain 1977).

The basic cloze may be a passage of general content or with content of a more technical nature, but relevant to the group of students. Generally, glosses are not given for difficult words appearing in the undeleted portion of the text, although the teacher may decide to gloss some such words at the margin or at the bottom of the page. Research has shown that giving target-language definitions or simpler synonyms for difficult vocabulary items does improve student scores (Moy 1975). In some settings, students are permitted to use a target-language or target-language/native-language dictionary when taking the cloze test to eliminate the problem of difficulty with words appearing in the undeleted portion of the text.[3]

One increasingly popular modification of the basic cloze test actually converts cloze into a fixed-response test: namely, the supplying of alternate-response choices for each blank in turn.[4] At least three varieties on this theme have been written up in the literature. There is the "alternate-choice" approach (Ozete 1977), wherein the student must choose from *two* words instead of a blank at random intervals; what has been termed the "maze" approach, where the student must choose from *three* words (Pikulski and Pikulski 1977); and the multiple-choice approach with *four* words to choose from (Jonz 1976). Generally, those who recommend one of these types of alternate-choice formats suggest that the best distractors are those obtained from answers to the same cloze passage when administered in the basic way. Others (e.g., Porter 1976) would generate distractors intuitively according to the reading level of the students—grammatically and semantically incorrect distractors for beginners, just semantically incorrect for intermediate students, and incorrect for style or register reasons with advanced students. Whether distractors are derived from student answers or derived intuitively with some rationale in mind (like Porter's), the provision of choices changes the nature of the task dramatically. Students no longer have to make such sweeping, global choices as to the nature of the missing word (e.g., conjunction, adverb, auxiliary verb), the appropriate choice semantically, syntactic agreement in the context, its fit in the thread of discourse beyond the phrase level, and so forth.

This discussion has concerned itself primarily with the validity of the multiple-choice cloze—i.e., whether it really assesses the reading of a passage as discourse. There is the further question as to its reliability. Some research findings indicate that the open-ended cloze is more reliable than a multiple-choice cloze—i.e., students are more likely to respond similarly on repeated testing using the former version of the test (Rand 1978). Efforts are under way, however, to produce reliable, standardized multiple-choice cloze tests (Ilyin, forthcoming).

What cloze can be used for

For one thing, cloze can be used to check the readability of foreign-language passages, just as it was first used to test the readability of native-language passages. Oller (1979) reviews the conventional readability formulas and points out that these formulas are restricted in what they measure—sentence length in words, number of unfamiliar words, and number of affixes—and that they are not very accurate because reading comprehension depends on all elements combined. He notes that sometimes increased sentence length may, in fact, help readability.

In using cloze as a readability measure for foreign-language tests, it has been suggested that if a group of foreign students have a mean score of over 53 percent correct on a passage, they are reading at the "independent" level—i.e., the passage is easy enough for them so that they could read it without the help of a teacher. If their score is between 44 and 53 percent correct on the cloze, the passage could be considered at the "instructional" level for these students—i.e., a passage that they could read with the help of a teacher. If students get less than 44 percent correct, this passage is considered at the "frustrational" level—i.e., too difficult even with the help of a teacher (Haskell 1976). Research suggests that the actual percentages vary somewhat. In other words, the instructional level may range from 38 to 50 percent to 47 to 61 percent (see Anderson 1976, pp. 110–111). Scoring for "exact-word" restoration will also affect the range, with scores using the exact-word approach being lower (see below).

Cloze can also be used to test global reading-comprehension skills. In this function, cloze is testing for the learner's awareness of textual constraints—i.e., phrase-level, sentence-level, and paragraph-level dependencies. The assumption here is that successful performance on cloze depends on the interrelation of sentences in the passage (Oller 1975, Chihara, Oller, Weaver, and Chávez-Oller 1977).

Cloze can also be used to check for an awareness of grammatical relationships. For an item to be correct, it usually has to be grammatically correct, which means that it displays grammatical agreement with other elements in the passage (tense, gender, number, person, or whatever). The rationale for scoring grammar is that clues as to cohesion in discourse are often signaled through inflections in the text. Take the following example:

> A person unfamiliar with intestinal diseases _____ apt to let symptoms go unnoticed.

The reader who chooses the word "are" for closure here most likely has decided that the copula verb refers to "diseases" and not to "person." In fact, this *too-local* reading is common to nonnative readers, and ungrammatical answers on a cloze test such as the one in the above example can provide clear evidence to this effect.

The cloze can also be used to diagnose particular learner problems. Although the teacher may not necessarily know if knowledge of grammar, vocabulary, or total meaning of a passage is responsible for performance on any given item (Carroll 1973), researchers have demonstrated that it is possible to obtain diagnostic information from the cloze. One study compared the performance of students on content words (words with a lexical or semantic function, like nouns and verbs) as opposed to structure words (words with a grammatical function, like prepositions, auxiliary verbs, conjunctions, and adverbs) (Berkoff 1976). The study also compared stronger with weaker students, and looked at differential performance by word class. For example, the students had most difficulty with completions involving certain adverbs, sentence connectors, and possessive pronouns. Also, the better students were reading for meaning and paying less attention to structure words. The weaker students, on the other hand, were more likely to look for places "to pick up a few points." They would thus fill in more structure words than content words and would get more structure words than content words correct proportionate to total numbers of each. Another study produced a rank ordering of answers by word class according to how easy they were to restore in a cloze passage. The finding was that the most difficult to supply were adjectives, then adverbs, nouns, verbs, prepositions, pronouns, with articles being the easiest (Hanzeli 1979).

The cloze test can also be used as a placement test in the classroom to determine the relative reading-comprehension levels of students. It can be used as an exercise to see if students have learned certain vocabulary and structures. For example, the teacher can write out a passage containing vocabulary and structures that have been covered and then delete every sixth or seventh word. Cloze can also be used as a measure of achievement and has, in fact, been reported to be a more sensitive measure of improvement in reading comprehension than the conventional reading-comprehension test (Oller 1979).

By setting a time limit for completing the cloze, the teacher can also obtain a measure of students' ability to read material and process it rapidly. The average time allotment for cloze is about 1 hour for a passage with 50 blanks. A test intended to tax the student's ability to read rapidly could be intended for completion in a shorter time proportionately.

What the cloze test measures

Three types of knowledge are called for in order to complete a cloze passage correctly—linguistic knowledge, textual knowledge, and knowledge of the world. To answer a given cloze item, it may be sufficient to have the appropriate linguistic knowledge, i.e., to select a semantically appropriate lexical item and to use it in a grammatically acceptable way (e.g., to inflect a deleted verb correctly for tense, person, and number or to inflect a deleted noun for number). Correctly answering a cloze item may also call for textual knowledge—i.e., perception of the cohesive relationship between that item and the rest of the sentence, paragraph, or text as a whole. The number of such items probably varies from text to text (e.g., items which require awareness of pronominal reference). Then, finally, cloze items may tap the respondent's knowledge of the world (unless such words are not deleted out of discretionary judgment). An example would be the reference to a particular century (see above)—e.g., "From the beginning of the _____ century, when the slave system began its geographic and demographic explosion. . .".

In that the cloze assesses linguistic, textual, and sometimes world knowledge, it can be termed a measure of general reading comprehension. There is, in fact, a substantial body of literature reporting impressive correlations between cloze results and results on more traditional tests of reading comprehension (see Anderson 1976, chapter 3, for a review of such studies). Cloze is also a measure of writing ability, especially of a person's ability to write grammatically, in that students must write words into the blanks and these words must be inflected correctly, as stated above (although they may be spelled incorrectly). Interestingly enough, research findings have shown and are continuing to show that the cloze is a good projective measure of other language skills. A series of correlational studies (Darnell 1968, Oller 1973, Hinofotis 1976, Shohamy 1978) have found that the cloze test correlates highly with tests of listening.

Researchers have recently added a dimension that other studies of cloze have lacked, namely, correlation of cloze with performance on an established test of speaking proficiency, the Foreign Service Institute (FSI) Oral Interview, which has subscales for accent, grammar, vocabulary, fluency, and comprehension. In one study, two judges obtained the FSI ratings. The judges' ratings for a heterogeneous group of ESL students (n=106) on the FSI correlated r = .63 with the students' performance on the cloze, which is a relatively high correlation (Hinofotis 1976). Interrater reliability on the Oral Interview scales was .88. The Oral Interview rating of one judge correlated at .72 with cloze, while the rating of the other judge correlated at .54. When looking at correlations of cloze with individual Oral Interview subtests, we note that the grammar subscale correlated most highly with cloze, then fluency, then comprehension, vocabulary, and accent, in that order.

Another study (Shohamy 1978), this time with 106 learners of Hebrew as a foreign language (HFL), found that the FSI Oral Interview ratings (across *three* judges) correlated r = .81 to .84 with performance on the cloze, considerably higher correlations than the ESL study had obtained. Furthermore, interrater reliability ranged from .94 to .99, also higher than in the ESL study. As in the ESL study, the cloze correlated most highly with the grammar subscale of the FSI Oral Interview and least with the subscale rating pronunciation (accent).

The explanation for relatively high correlation between cloze and speaking is that both call for integrative performance. Taking a cloze test requires that students sort through their store of linguistic knowledge of the basic elements of the target language (grammar and vocabulary), as well as their sense of contextual appropriateness in order to produce a correct response. In speaking, a learner must do similar processing. True, in speech, learners have more freedom of choice regarding the elements that will appear in their utterance, but certain grammatical, lexical, and discourse constraints operate in speech as well.

Scoring and evaluating a cloze test

Scoring the cloze can be quite simple if the teacher gives credit only for restoration of the exact word in its correct form. Another approach is referred to as "scoring for contextual appropriateness" (Oller 1979). There is some variation in what this type of scoring implies. For example, in one approach called the "any-contextually-acceptable-answer" method, the word must be grammatically correct but incorrect spellings are not penalized (Aitken 1977).[5] Another approach disginguishes "acceptable restorations" (grammatical and correctly spelled) from "sensible restorations" (not necessarily grammatical or spelled correctly, but making sense in the context of the passage) (Cooper and Fishman 1977). For the purposes of the following discussion, we are referring to the "acceptable-word" method, which reflects the former approach, not the latter.

The use of a scoring system based on contextual appropriateness is not so easy to use but is crucial in a classroom setting where students get their papers back. Actually, research on cloze has found very high correlations between results using the acceptable and the exact scoring method (e.g., $r = .97$ in Stubbs and Tucker 1974), so that statistically the exact scoring method accomplishes the same purpose. The problem is that this approach is not psychologically palatable enough to teachers or to students. The raw score on cloze using the acceptable-word approach is initially low relative to a score on a traditional reading-comprehension test (see Bormuth 1967) but becomes still lower using the exact-restoration approach. This section will, in fact, discuss how the raw scores should be interpreted. Since the acceptable-word approach to scoring is being recommended for classroom purposes, this section will also discuss some of the scoring problems that teachers are faced with.

The acceptable-word approach to scoring has both semantic and grammatical components. The semantic component is not easy to deal with. By leaving out blanks, the teacher is in essence giving the student an opportunity to produce a correct collocation (juxtaposition of words) for the given environment, and sometimes it is difficult for a native reader (scorer) to judge whether a given collocation produced by a student is acceptable or not. It is useful to give the cloze passage to natives of the target language to fill out. Usually there is general agreement among them as to acceptable answers. These answers can serve as the basis for an answer key. The problem is that learners of the target language often supply answers that natives never would have used but which are acceptable or marginally acceptable.

It also happens that as teachers keep encountering the same questionable form on a number of papers, they may begin to consider the form acceptable. In fact, this is one of the various ways in which previously unacceptable forms or collocations in a language eventually become acceptable to native speakers—i.e., through repeated exposure to them. So there is a problem of scorer reliability here—of being consistent in marking. It may be that the teacher should check back over the scoring after all the papers are corrected to make sure that the same answer is not marked correct in one place and incorrect in another.

The area of grammatical correctness is more straightforward but is also an area of debate in scoring the cloze. Some teachers feel that scoring for grammatical precision is unnecessary. After all, points are not taken off for spelling. Particularly in courses where students are not taught to write and not generally evaluated on their productive skills, it appears unnecessary to grade for grammar. The problem is that an awareness of grammatical markings is an important part of the reading process and such markings may be indicators of cohesion in the text, as pointed out above.

It is argued that at least there should be differential weighting for grammatical errors of different magnitude. For example, perhaps omission of the *s* in "he *eat* lunch" is a lower-order error than omitting the *ed* marker for past tense in "he *walk* home yesterday." Yet there are multiple problems with this approach. First, it is difficult to know where to draw the line—what to weigh more than what. A seemingly simple grammatical inflection may have a complex function within the context of discourse. Also, the use of a weighting scheme makes scoring more complicated. Items of a grammatical nature tend not to be of high frequency altogether in a cloze passage, maybe 10 to 15 percent in all (according to several calculations that I have made). What about the use of forms that *are* acceptable in some nonstandard dialect? It is up to the teacher to decide how nonstandard the forms are and whether to accept them.

There have been several recent efforts to assess the acceptability of answers by detailed, objective categories (Clarke and Burdell 1977, Nir and Blum-Kulka, in press), rather than by broad, more subjective categories (as suggested by Bowen 1969, Oller et al. 1972). One scoring system specifies the way in which credit is to be given if students satisfy *some* of the constraints in their answers (Clarke and Burdell 1977). The "code sheet" includes a scale for "syntactic acceptability" (4–0), "semantic acceptability" (6–0), and "semantic change" (to be used if 6 on "semantic acceptability"; 3–0).[6] The authors admit that this scheme requires "substantial investment of time and effort." Another, somewhat less complex scheme developed by Nir and Blum-Kulka (in press) is used to analyze cloze results presented below.

Once the cloze is scored, there is the further issue of how to evaluate the results. It is important for teachers to realize that students are not expected to achieve high grades on most cloze tests. As mentioned above, student scores of between 44 and 53 percent correct on a cloze passage may well indicate that the passage is just at the appropriate level of difficulty for that class (Haskell 1976). Some research on young native speakers of English, for example, suggests that a score of 43 percent on a cloze is comparable to a score of 75 percent on a standard multiple-choice test of reading comprehension (Bormuth 1967).

A cloze test as an example

It seems that a meaningful way to discuss scoring would be actually to go through the exercise of completing a cloze. The following is a cloze passage with 100 blanks to fill in, with approximately seven or eight words between blanks. The passage was administered as an end-of-fall-trimester exam to 370 social science students taking English as a foreign language in their first year at the Hebrew University of Jerusalem. The course concentrates on reading skills, and particularly on the handling of lengthy reading lists. Thus the cloze passage is relatively long. Students were given 60 minutes to complete the cloze and were allowed to use a dictionary (English-Hebrew or English-English).

* * * * * *

Fill out the cloze test below and try to pay attention to the tasks that you are performing. Note the instances in which filling in of blanks is dependent on not just the immediate context but the larger context of the passage. For example, note the importance of backward and forward reference—how certain blanks involve simply the repetition of some word that precedes or follows it.

SAMPLE CLOZE

INSTRUCTIONS
In the following passage 100 words have been omitted. Read the passage and insert whatever word makes sense according to the meaning of the passage. The word should be grammatically correct. Remember—insert only ONE word in each space. Read the whole passage at least once before you start to write.

Example: The boy   _walked_   across the street and bumped
                              (a)

  into   a lamppost. He   _was_   shaken up a little, but he
     (b)   (c)

managed to   _continue_   walking.
                      (d)

The Jet Age Malady

A U.S. male brought up on the East Coast of America stands eighteen to twenty inches away from another male when in conversation. In talking to a woman he will increase the distance by about four inches. To stand at a distance of about thirteen inches usually has a sexual or aggressive connotation. However, in most parts of Latin America thirteen _____ is just the right distance when talking
                                    (1)
_____ a person. When a man brought up in a _____ American
  (2)   (3)
environment tries to talk to a _____ brought up on the East Coast
                                  (4)
of _____ United States an interesting thing happens. The Latin will
    (5)
_____ to maintain what he considers the _____ talking
  (6)   (7)
distance. The American will, of course, step _____ . Both will feel
                                              (8)
uncomfortable without quite _____ why. All they know is that
                              (9)

_____ is something wrong with the other_____. Most
(10)   (11)
culture-blind Latins feel that the Americans_____withdrawn
                                              (12)
and uncommunicative. Most culture-blind Americans _____
                                                    (13)
that Latins are pushy.

In most American urban areas, _____ be two minutes
                               (14)
_____ for an appointment is all right. Three _____ is sig-
(15)   (16)
nificant, but an apology is not expected. _____ five minutes the
                                           (17)
latecomer mutters an apology. In _____ Latin countries a five
                                  (18)
minute unit is not _____ : an apology is expected only for a time
                    (19)
_____ longer than twenty minutes. Latins, influenced by
(20)
_____ own cultural conditioning, feel that Americans are
(21)
_____ polite and are obsessed with time because they_____
(22)   (23)
persons with whom they have appointments to _____ at a certain
                                              (24)
place at precisely a _____ time. A person unfamiliar with North
                      (25)
American cultural conditioning _____ difficulty realizing that
                                (26)
Americans handle time much_____some tangible material—
                           (27)
spending it, taking _____ , using it up, or wasting it. _____ a
                     (28)   (29)
Spanish-American or a Spaniard comes to work _____ he says,
                                              (30)
"El bus me dejó" ("The bus _____ me"), as opposed to the
                            (31)
American " _____ missed the bus." In English, the clock "runs."
            (32)
_____ Spanish "El reloj anda" (the clock walks).
(33)

Different _____ live almost literally in different worlds,
(34)
_____ just the same world with different _____ attached.
(35)   (36)
The barriers between cultures _____ perhaps be relatively
(37)
unimportant if only _____ handful of people were crossing inter-
(38)
national _____ . But people the world over are on _____
(39)   (40)
move today as never before, _____ for business and, more and
(41)
more, for the _____ of seeing and experiencing other ways of
(42)
_____ . All this has its obvious benefits. _____ the same time,
(43)   (44)
however, there are _____ dangers, particularly for a person
(45)
_____ plans to spend any appreciable amount of _____ in
(46)   (47)
another culture. One of these dangers _____ the sense of
(48)
confusion and misunderstanding _____ social psychologists call
(49)
culture shock.

A person _____ enters a foreign culture ordinarily passes
(50)
_____ three phases of adjustment. First, he _____ a spec-
(51)   (52)
tator; he observes what is _____ on around him but does not
(53)
_____ . Second, he becomes personally involved in the _____
(54)   (55)
of the foreign culture and tries to _____ to terms with them.
(56)
Finally, _____ he will have mastered the new situation and
(57)
_____ get along smoothly in the new _____ or he will realize
(58)   (59)
that his _____ culture is the only workable one for _____ .
(60)   (61)

In the first phase, that of _____ , the initial reaction to a new
(62)
_____ is likely to be one of curiosity_____ delight. Every-
(63)   (64)
thing looks interesting. However, a _____ weeks' time changes
(65)
one's perception of the _____ . Living in a country is quite differ-
(66)
ent _____ just visiting it. As the person _____ to move into
(67)   (68)
the _____ and most difficult phase, that of participation and
(69)
_____ involvement in the unfamiliar culture, he _____
(70)   (71)
aware of the great differences that _____ between himself and the
(72)
people with _____ he is living. The situations which, _____
(73)   (74)
his first phase as spectator, were _____ are now incompre-
(75)
hensible and perhaps even _____ . He feels that he cannot "get
(76)
through" to _____ , and he becomes uneasy and insecure
(77)
_____ he doesn't know the right _____ of doing things.
(78)   (79)
Culture shock is precipitated by the distressing _____ of
(80)
uncertainty and anxiety that result from _____ finding all the
(81)
familiar symbols, signs, and cues that _____ a person through his
(82)
own culture. He _____ himself having to use a _____
(83)   (84)
"design for living." He doesn't know what people _____ of him
(85)
and what he should expect of _____ . He is not at all sure
(86)
_____ to shake hands, how much to tip, _____ to buy things
(87)   (88)
he needs, _____ what to say to waiters, and he _____ that the
(89)   (90)

social etiquette he has _____ is no longer of use to him.
(91)

_____ shock is usually accompanied by a linguistic _____
(92)   (93)

that makes it even more difficult to _____ the cultural barriers.
(94)

When I was _____ linguistic shock, English sentences would
(95)

sound to _____ like a long, unpronounceable string of harsh
(96)

_____ . At that time I deeply regretted the _____ that I had
(97)   (98)

chosen to learn English _____ of some sensible language. I
(99)

couldn't see why the _____ people had to use these odd,
(100)

barbaric utterances instead of speaking with normal human words

like everyone else. I sometimes had the feeling that Americans spoke

English in order to confuse unsuspecting foreigners.

✳ ✳ ✳ ✳ ✳ ✳

After filling out the cloze, check your answers with those provided
on the answer sheet that follows. Make note of instances where your
answer was not one of the suggested answers on the answer sheet.

Suggested Answers to "The Jet Age Malady" Cloze

1. inches
2. with, to
3. Latin, South
4. person, man
5. the
6. try, attempt
7. right, correct, normal,
   proper, ideal, best, usual,
   suitable
8. back, backwards, aside
9. knowing, realizing,
   understanding
10. there

11. person, one, man, side,
    fellow
12. are
13. feel, think
14. to
15. late
16. minutes
17. After
18. most, many, the, some
19. significant, important,
    appreciable
20. unit, span, lapse, period,
    much

21. their
22. not
23. expect
24. be
25. given
26. has
27. like
28. it
29. If, When
30. late
31. left
32. I
33. In
34. societies, peoples
35. not
36. names, labels, values
37. would, could
38. a
39. borders
40. the
41. traveling, mainly
42. purpose, fun, pleasure
43. life, living
44. At
45. some, certain, obvious
46. who
47. time
48. is
49. that
50. who
51. through
52. is
53. going
54. participate
55. ways
56. come
57. either
58. will
59. culture, environment
60. own
61. him

62. spectator, observer, observation
63. country, culture
64. and
65. few
66. environment, scene
67. from
68. begins
69. second
70. personal, total
71. becomes
72. exist
73. whom, who
74. during, in
75. interesting, delightful
76. unpleasant, absurd, etc.
77. them, people, anyone, others
78. because
79. way, ways, method
80. feelings, presence
81. not
82. guide, guided, help
83. finds
84. different, foreign, new
85. expect, think
86. them
87. when, how
88. where, how
89. or (and)
90. finds, discovers
91. learned
92. Culture
93. shock, deficit
94. cross, overcome
95. suffering, experiencing, undergoing, in
96. me
97. noises, sounds
98. fact, day
99. instead
100. English, American

Usually, native speakers of the language are in general agreement over appropriate responses because native speakers have a shared set of expectancies about closure. Responses from foreign students, however, may be far removed from what any native speaker would provide but may still be plausible.

In the study of student responses to the first twenty items,[7] certain patterns emerged as to why items were wrong. Concurrent work by Nir and Blum-Kulka (in press) helped me to refine my categorization of the patterns. These researchers have designed a taxonomy for interpreting deviant cloze responses. Their taxonomy includes (1) the type of deviation from the word in the original (e.g., lexical/semantic, grammatical, or orthographic), (2) the level at which the response is unacceptable (micro- or macro-level), and (3) the likelihood that the respondent understood this portion of the text despite the error. It should be understood that the *micro-context* refers to the immediate context of the blank (i.e., the word, words, or phrase that the deleted word is immediately associated with) and the *macro-context* refers to the sentence, paragraph, section, or total passage. The following discussion of response patterns makes use of this taxonomy.

Micro-context: grammatically unacceptable.   Sometimes the student supplied a word that would have been correct had the word class been appropriate. For example, in 7, "the _____ talking distance," the noun "conversation" was marked as wrong but would probably have been considered correct as the adjective "conversational" in a "conversational talking distance," although this phrase would sound somewhat redundant.

There were several examples of grammatical errors of inflection. In 9, "without quite _____ why," several students supplied "know" or "understand," omitting the present participial inflection -*ing*. Also, most likely because of interference from the native language (Hebrew) which allows omission of the copula ("to be") in present tense, students responded to 12, "Americans _____ withdrawn and uncommunicative," with "people" or "males," instead of "are." Either they did not notice the plural marker on "Americans," or they just perceived it as modifying "people," since in Hebrew the adjective is pluralized to agree with a plural noun. Another example of inferred deletion of the copula occurred in 20 ("for a time _____ longer than twenty minutes"), for which 17 students supplied "which" or "that," the way in which the utterances would be said in Hebrew.

Another micro-level grammatical problem regarded the surrogate subject *there* in 10. Several students supplied "it," the other surrogate subject, and others simply ignored it and supplied an adverb like "maybe" or "sometimes," a common type of error for nonnative learners of English from a number of language backgrounds (see, for example, Burt and Kiparsky 1972, p. 13).

Micro-context: lexically/semantically unacceptable.   Frequently students would supply a word from the same word class in a related semantic range, but inappropriate for the particular micro-context. For example, "male" instead of "person" in 4 was not accepted in that it was too precise a reference to sex. For 6 ("The Latin will _____ to maintain what he considers the __right__ talking distance...") "tend" was not accepted in place of "try" or "attempt," in that "tend" was thought to weaken the statement too much, while "have" was not accepted in that it made the statement too strong. Here we see some grounds for debate as to acceptability of response. In 19 ("In __most__ Latin countries a five-minute unit is not _____") we really see where semantic limits at the level of micro-context become fuzzy. "Significant," "important," and "appreciable" were accepted, but not "serious," "long," or "much." The decision was made to accept only answers indicating the significance of the delay. Therefore, "long" and "much" are not specific enough. "Serious" in that context is close but would call for a slightly different context—e.g., "being five minutes late is not __serious__ ." These examples suggest that deciding where to draw the line is not always easy.

Macro-context: lexical/semantic.   Students provided a fill-in that made an acceptable collocation in the micro-context but was incorrect given the macro-context of the sentence or section. For example, in 3, a local answer was " __west/new/another__ American," instead of " __Latin__ American," as called for by the passage. In 9, if students responded "quite odd" instead of "knowing" ("without quite __knowing__ why"), they were displaying a particularly local, micro-level reading and response strategy.

Sometimes students provided an answer that was the complete opposite of what was called for, thus exhibiting an inability to pick up contextual clues from the macro-context. For example, in 8 ("The American will, of course, step __back/aside__ "), a student answered "nearer," despite the textual references to Latins, not North Americans, standing nearer (the reference to "thirteen inches" in 1) and to

Americans seeming withdrawn (12). A few students also demonstrated lack of comprehension by supplying "no" or "not" for 20—"a time ___unit/span___ longer than twenty minutes." Their response is in opposition to the thrust of the point, which is that only being *more* than twenty minutes late for a meeting is cause for an apology.

Native-speaker difficulties with the passage.   Note that native speakers of the language may not get 100 percent on a cloze such as the one presented here. I, personally, missed five items, partly because I did the test rapidly and somewhat carelessly (taking perhaps only 10 of the allotted 60 minutes). The first two that I got wrong were 23 and 24. Here is an example of how difficult items can be so closely interlinked that if one is wrong the other will be, too. In "they _____ persons with whom they have appointments to _____ at a certain place . . . ," I filled in "have" and "keep," respectively, rather than "expect" and "be." For 27, I gave a local answer, "as," rather than "like," in that I saw "much" and immediately thought "as much as." For 35, I supplied "albeit" rather than "not," thus shifting the meaning and producing a somewhat awkward form. Finally, out of carelessness I made a local error on 44, "all" instead of "at," since I read "_____ the same" and did not notice the word "time" after "same" ("_____ the same time"). The fact that natives do have some difficulty completing a cloze task simply underscores the reality that this pragmatic testing approach does tax the powers of concentration and range of reading ability not only of the second-language learner but of natives as well.

Dictation

It is easy to conceive of dictation tests simply as contextualized spelling tests because the traditional use of dictation has been to see whether students can spell in their native language or in another language. In such tests, the passage is subdivided into relatively small chunks and the teacher reads these chunks at a slow, purposely unnatural pace, in order to give students an opportunity to focus their attention on correct spelling forms and punctuation.

The use of dictation in testing functional language ability is a departure from the traditional approach in several basic ways. First, the chunks of discourse are longer—perhaps 7 to 10 words per chunk, as opposed to 3 to 5 in the more traditional method. Pauses occur as much as possible at natural pause boundaries. The material is presented at a normal rate of speech. The length of the pause between chunks may be varied in order to make the task easier or more difficult. Punctuation is supplied, as is paragraphing. The dictation is scored according to word-for-word correspondence. Spelling is ignored unless the spelling of a word affects the meaning of the word (e.g., "write" instead of "right," "long" instead of "wrong").

The theory behind what might be called "pragmatic dictation" is that the act of segmenting the sound chain calls for an active, dynamic process of analysis-by-synthesis (Oller 1972). As Oller (1979) puts it, "The reason that dictation works well is that the whole family of auditory tasks that it comprises faithfully reflect crucial aspects of the very activities that one must normally perform in processing discourse auditorily." In his new book, Oller provides an extensive discussion of different formats for dictation tests. Here, we will limit our discussion to the "standard" dictation format, wherein the students listen to a passage and reproduce the entire passage in writing.

The use of a conversational rate of delivery with chunks of sufficient length to challenge the examinee's short-term memory is intended to make the dictation task approximate certain other tasks that learners are asked to perform in their everyday use of the language. One such task is note taking. Students hear information, try to process it accurately, and write down what they have heard. It is true that in real communicative situations, the learner may write down only the essence of what has been heard or even write down a translation of salient points, whereas the dictation task calls for complete and exact reproduction of what is said. But unlike the typical lecture-hall situation, telephone call, or whatever, the learner is given three opportunities to hear the dictated material, the second time with pauses between chunks of information. Such repetition is a "luxury" in the real world, particularly when student listeners are unable to stop a lecturer, say, every time they have a question as to what the lecturer has said.

As in the case of the cloze test, pragmatic dictation tests have been shown to be good predictors of total performance on a language-proficiency battery (Oller 1972). Also, EFL teachers have found dictation to be diagnostic of different types of learner problems with English-language structures, such as verb tense (Cohen 1975a). Research is beginning to appear relating the integrative type of dictation to the specific kinds of items and procedures found in reading-comprehension tests. It has been found, for example, that dictation seems to measure lower-order skills rather than the higher-order skills of inference and the like measured in comprehension tests (Alderson 1978). This line of investigation may prove valuable in identifying more precisely the actual integrative skills being measured by such a test.

Choosing the dictation passage

A dictation may be written by the teacher, using material that is known to be suited to the students' level of overall language proficiency, it may be a paraphrase of familiar material, or it may simply be a selected passage from a student textbook.

It is important that the passage be at least 100 words long so that it is possible to assess performance in connected discourse. There are no absolute criteria for deciding where to put the pauses in the dictation passage, but breaks should be spaced so as to require processing of the material at the level of meaning, rather than simply at the phonetic-unit level. Such decisions will depend on the level of the students.

Administration procedures

Usually the text is read once at a conversational rate while the students just listen. The second time it is read with pauses at the determined points and with punctuation supplied, as it appears in the text. The third time the passage is read through normally or with slight pauses at the selected points, while the examinees check what they have written. Students are told at the outset that punctuation and paragraphing will be given and they are briefed as to the names for the necessary punctuation marks—period, comma, semicolon, etc.

Scoring and evaluating a dictation test

A dictation exercise is relatively easy to score because it has a fixed structure. There is only one area where "acceptable answers" become a problem. That is the area of spelling. The pragmatic dictation does not test for spelling, for several reasons. One is that even natives have trouble spelling, especially in English, where sound-symbol correspondence is not always close. Another reason is that general spelling errors may not be so numerous proportionate to other types of errors. On dictation in English, Oller (1979) reports that a group of 145 foreign students averaged only 1½ spelling errors per dictation, whereas they made an average of 50 or more other types of errors. Oller also found that proficiency in English spelling among foreign students does not correlate highly with overall proficiency.[8]

Given, then, that the pragmatic dictation exercise does not score for spelling, the issue is one of where to draw the line—how to distinguish between a spelling error and a structural error. For example, in the third sentence of the dictation presented below ("in a city where the pedestrian has the right of way . . ."), what if the student writes "ride" instead of "right"? The student may, in fact, be spelling phonetically, because the final *t* is more like a voiced *d* before the schwa vowel in "of." Is this then a spelling problem or a structural problem? For the sake of consistency, a rule of thumb is to ask if a native speaker would make this mistake. If "ride" instead of "right" does not reflect a native-like mistake, it would be scored as an error. The truth is that such decisions are somewhat arbitrary nonetheless. The important thing is for the teacher to mark all students the same way.

The scoring is done on a word for word basis. Experience has shown that learners are found to alter dictated material in one of four ways—by (1) adding new elements, (2) deleting elements, (3) substituting one element for another, or (4) transposing the order of elements. If, as occasionally happens, students add a new word or phrase in writing their version of the dictation, this addition is circled as one error. If one or more elements are deleted, the teacher inserts a caret at the place of deletion and places a little circle above the line for each deleted word. If elements are substituted for the correct element, the teacher circles these. If, for instance, two words are written instead of the one required (e.g., "best friends" for "pedestrians"), the two words are circled as one error. A word or phrase transposed to another position is circled as one error, with an arrow directed to its appropriate position.

Capitalization errors are ignored, as are punctuation errors—including the apostrophe for possessive and for contractions. If all or most of the students appear to have contracted a form that was supposedly dictated in its full form, for example, the teacher may want to consider the possibility that he dictated it in the contracted form. For this reason, teachers may wish to tape the dictation rather than giving it orally. (Or they could dictate it orally and make a recording of themselves as well, in order to check later as to how they actually uttered certain forms.) Students argue that a dictation is easier if it is possible to see the teacher's mouth moving, but learners are often in pragmatic situations where they cannot see the mouth movements of the person whose output they are writing down—e.g., input from the telephone, from the radio, or from a lecturer in a large lecture hall. So this recorded format is not so artificial.

It is important to take into consideration that the delivery of the dictation will affect the results. Speed and level of formality will determine whether fast speech rules go into effect, for example, thus influencing what the student hears—e.g., the phrase [raydəwey] in rapid speech as opposed to [rayt əv wey] "right of way" in exaggeratedly slow speech. My own bias is for the most natural delivery in the given situation.[9] For a lecture-type delivery, this would mean relatively fast speech. However, for the sake of analyzability, the dictation would not include false starts and filled pauses.

As to assigning points, teachers have an option. They can simply count up the words in the dictation and make this the total score, since scoring is on a one-to-one basis. Thus, if a dictation has 75 words, the total score is also 75. Or if the dictation is part of a larger test in which the dictation has been alloted, say, 15 points, then each error would be scaled down to 0.2 of a point (i.e., $15 \div 75 = 0.2$). Thus a student who got a score of 60 on the dictation would have an adjusted score of 12 (i.e., $60 \times 0.2 = 12$).

A dictation test as an example

The following is a sample dictation as it appeared in the 1973 University of California, Los Angeles, English Entrance Exam:

* * * * * *

DICTATION

Instructions: You will be given a dictation passage. The passage will be read once at normal speed. Just listen. The second time, the passage will be read with pauses between word groups and you are to write down what you hear. The passage will be read a third time at normal speed. Check over your work during this reading. Punctuation will be given during the slow reading. A period is the same as a full stop ("."). Spelling and punctuation will not be graded.

It is often observed / that pedestrians are a peculiar sight / along the streets of Los Angeles. / Most residents of this vast city / prefer traveling to their destination by car / to going there on foot. / In fact, it is ironic / that in a city where the pedestrian / has the right of way, / there aren't very many pedestrians / around to take it. / People who do go out walking / frequently turn out to be tourists. / Imagine the surprise /

when the individual seeking directions / learns that the fellow pedestrian / from whom he has sought directions / is also a stranger in town. / / (The slashes indicate where pauses were supplied.)

* * * * * *

The following were the instructions to the teachers scoring the exams:

> Correct only for structural mistakes, e.g., verb tenses, subject-verb agreement, number, prepositions. Take off 1/3 point for each mistake. Do not correct for punctuation or spelling. Distinguish between misspelled words like "ocasion" and structural errors like "prefer" for "prefers," "honor" for "honored," "fortunate" for "fortunately."
>
> Take off a maximum of 15 points for this dictation. Round off the final score— 12 2/3 = 13, 10 1/3 = 10, etc.

We see that in this case the maximum score was not the total number of words (97), but rather *15,* the number of points allotted to this subtest on a total 100-point exam. Each error was given 1/3 on the basis of previous pilot testing,[10] which indicated that this was the weighting that best produced a spread of student scores from 0 to 15. If the scorer could identify 45 errors right away, without line-by-line analysis, the student received no credit for the dictation.

I composed this dictation, rather than extracting it from a book, in order to include a series of structures intended to tax the students' powers of language storage and reproduction. The passage has various types of subordinate clauses and employs vocabulary words intended to assess the learners' powers of identification and discrimination. Many of these words had proved troublesome to students on previous dictations used in UCLA placement examinations. The passage was piloted on several groups of students before being revised for use in the form appearing here.

Although it can be argued that a dictation loses some of its natural, pragmatic quality when it is composed by the teacher rather than being found in its natural state, there are some real advantages to composed texts. If the teachers have elements in mind that they would like to test for, they may have difficulty finding an already-existing passage that combines these various elements. Of course, if teachers write their own passage, it would pay for them to check the passage with one or more native speakers to make sure that it sounds natural. In an effort to be inclusive, teachers may generate sentences that sound somewhat forced.

A simulated response to the above dictation is shown below. This response which could have been that of a student is given in order to show scoring procedures. Score it yourself; check it against the scoring and explanation provided.

In scoring this student's dictation, we will use symbols to indicate each of the types of errors. They are as follows:

addition	= A
deletion	= D
substitution	= S
transposition	= T

In this system, then, a spelling error that changes the structure of the word—grammatically or semantically—is also a substitution.

✶ ✶ ✶ ✶ ✶ ✶

PASSAGE TO SCORE

It is often observe pedestrian is a peculiar side along streets of Los Angeles. Most residents of this city prefer to travel their destiny by car to go there on the foot. It is in fact very ironik that a city where the pedestrian has the way of right, aren't very many pedestrians around to take it. People who go walking frekwently turn out to be turist. Imagen the suprise when the individual seeking direction learn that the fellow pedestrian from who he has sot directions is also the stranger in town.

SUGGESTED SCORING

It is often observe pedestrian is a pecular side along streets of

Los Angeles. Most residents of this city prefer to travel their

destiny by car to go there on the foot. It is in fact very ironik

that a city where the pedestrian has the way of right aren't very

many pedestrians around to take it. People who go walking

frekwently turn out to be turist. Imagen the surprise when the individual seeking directio$\underset{D}{\overset{O}{n}}$ lear$\underset{D}{\overset{O}{n}}$ that the fellow pedestrian

from wh$\underset{D}{\overset{O}{o}}$ he has sot directions is also(the)stranger in town.

* * * * * *

There are 24 errors in this student's response, if we count as one error the double transposition, "way of right" for "right of way." Using the 1/3-off per error method, 8 points would be taken off out of 15, producing a score of 7. If the score were based simply on total words, it would be 97 minus the 24 errors, or 73. Another way is to convert the number of words correct to a percentage—hence 73 out of 97 = 75 percent.

It is always a good idea to keep referring back to the original dictation while scoring papers, even after the passage seems to be memorized. This is in order to catch errors of deletion. Such errors can easily be overlooked in scoring, particularly when they are not essential (e.g., "very" in "very many pedestrians").

Dialog

There are now a fair number of tests for measuring oral language proficiency in a second or foreign language, many of which have been prompted by the advent of bilingual schooling on the North American continent. Whereas just five years ago there were only a few instruments intended for use with children (see Cohen 1975d), a recent book evaluating oral language tests for bilingual students (Silverman, Noa, and Russell 1976) now provides reviews of over a dozen instruments that assess oral language in at least two languages. There are also several structured interview measures intended particularly for assessing second-language speaking among adults, such as the Ilyin Oral Interview (Ilyin 1976), the Oral Communication Test (English Language Institute, University of Michigan), and the Foreign Service Institute (FSI) Oral Interview Technique (all discussed in detail in Oller 1979). The FSI test appears to be one of the most highly valued external measures for assessing speaking skill, and in fact, a special conference was recently devoted in part to discussing aspects of the FSI test (Clark 1978).

Oral-proficiency tests become tests of functional or pragmatic speaking ability when (and only when) they "afford opportunities for examinees to display their ability to string sequences of elements in a stream of speech in appropriate correspondence with extralinguistic context" (Oller 1979). Oller indicates that for a test to be rated as pragmatic, the scoring technique must relate to "the totality of the discourse-level meanings and not exclusively to discrete points of morphology or syntax." Thus, for an already-existing oral-language measure to be pragmatic in nature, it may be necessary to modify both the data-collection procedures and the specified scoring procedures. For example, the teacher would replace a score for grammatical accuracy with a score for contextual appropriateness (or simply add on the latter). In a question-answer format type of test, for example, a student's answer would be scored for whether it made sense in the context and provided everything necessary to answer the question adequately (regardless of whether it was grammatical).

Taking this approach, then, there is no *one* design for a pragmatic speaking test, as we might speak of a fixed-ratio cloze test or of a pragmatic test of dictation. Rather, the classroom teacher is free to use a variety of techniques, such as those enumerated in Chapter 4 under Item-Response Formats. There is also a recent EFL book by Dubin and Margol (1977) which provides ideas for 200 or so different situationally-based communication activities. It would be possible to include in such activities notionally-based exchanges as well—e.g., involving requests, promises, apologies, and so forth.

A rating scale for assessing pragmatic speaking in the classroom

In her book on communicative ability in a second language, Savignon (1972) provided four communicative settings for the purposes of assessing functional speaking ability: discussing a topic with a native speaker of the second language, interviewing a native speaker as if for a newspaper article, reporting facts about oneself or one's recent activities, and describing what someone is doing. Jakobovits and Gordon (1974, pp. 49–55) add two more communicative activities for testing what they refer to as "transactional competence":[11] being funny in the second language while being accurate and informative about a topic (e.g., family life), and relating the contents of a conversation between two second-language speakers.

Subsequent efforts include that of Levenston (1975), who devised a series of 60 situations in order to assess the language learner's "ability to function in face-to-face speech situations." The students were asked to imagine that they were in the situation that is described. They were told what had happened so far and were to say what they felt was suitable. Sample situations included:

1. There is a very nice girl in your English class and you would like to have coffee with her after class.
2. You are in a restaurant. The plate you are given by the waiter is dirty.
3. You are driving your car in a 30 miles-per-hour speed limit zone. A police car stops you and the policeman says you were traveling at 40 miles per hour.

It is important to consider the way in which such data are elicited (i.e., the item-stimulus format). Some stimuli are more open-ended than others. Levenston's "situations" are more structured in nature than Savignon's or Jakobovits and Gordon's tasks. Such differences may affect student output. It may also be that certain tasks call for more of a role-playing ability than other tasks. But the *crucial* issue appears to be one of how the data are treated. Levenston suggests a simple 3-point marking system: (1) appropriate in "form" (i.e., the native speaker's way of expressing the message) and in "content" (i.e., the native speaker's message in the given situation), (2) appropriate in content but *not* in form, or (3) inappropriate in content (and then, whether the *form* is appropriate becomes irrelevant). Thus, if the student responds to situation 1 above (inviting a girl to have coffee) with, "Would you be free to have coffee with me after class?" he would be marked correct for form and content. If in situation 2 (dirty plate in restaurant), he said, "Because this plate is dirty, I wish that you would exchange it," he would get credit for content but not for form, because according to Levenston's research findings, no natives used the conjunction "because" in this situation. They said things like, "Would you change this plate, please? It's dirty." As to situation 3 (being stopped for speeding), if the student replies, "Can you prove it?" or "You're crazy," as foreign students did in Levenston's study, such responses were marked as inappropriate in content. One could argue that this is a case of inappropriate form rather than content—in other words, that it *is* acceptable to disagree with a policeman's judgment, but that the speaker would do it differently. For example, he would say, "I don't think so," or "Are you sure?" or something of that nature. In other words, he might well indulge in bickering with the policeman (content) but would use some other form for the message. A clear case of violation of content in the United States, for example, might be to ask someone at a party how much he paid for his house or how much he makes a month. This is perfectly acceptable in some parts of the world.

Both Savignon (1972) and Jakobovits and Gordon (1974) provide more detailed categories than does Levenston for scoring the ability to function in face-to-face speech situations. Levenston (personal communication) reports that he kept his rating scheme less detailed because the more elaborate the less reliable.

A suggested rating scale

Let us now consider a suggested integration of the three above-mentioned scoring schemes into one (Table 1). This scheme is not intended as an exhaustive scheme but rather as a basis for classroom use by teachers. I have used Levenston's basic division between form and content. The dimension of *form* is broken down into three rating scales: (1) *naturalness of discourse*—whether the learner selects and orders discourse elements appropriately—i.e., realizes speech acts in

Table 1   Rating Scale for Pragmatic Speaking

		FORM						
1.	Naturalness of discourse:	unnatural	1	2	3	4	5	natural
2.	Style of expression:	foreign	1	2	3	4	5	native
3.	Clarity of expression:	unclear	1	2	3	4	5	clear
		CONTENT						
4.	Suitability:	unsuitable	1	2	3	4	5	suitable
5.	Accuracy of information:	inaccurate	1	2	3	4	5	accurate
6.	Amount of information related:	inappropriate (too little, too much)	1	2	3	4	5	appropriate

an acceptable way within the flow of discourse (see, for example, Coulthard 1977; also Fraser 1979); (2) *style of expression*—whether the learner uses acceptable stylistic devices by native standards. For example, the learner may use a passive verb form in a context where a native would use the active form; (3) *clarity of expression, comprehensibility*—whether the learner's use of forms makes for a readily interpretable message.

The dimension of *content* is also broken down into three rating scales: (4) *suitability*—whether learners use the native speaker's message in the given situation; whether they adhere to accepted socio-cultural rules of use. The rating of suitability is based on a number of variables—native culture, age of speakers, sex, social class, occupation, roles in the interaction, status, and so forth. The best rule of thumb is just a gut feeling for whether the content could be native-like taking the above variables (especially peer language and register) into consideration; (5) *accuracy of information*—whether in reporting or describing something, the learner is able to convey each idea, statement, or action accurately; (6) *amount of information related*— whether the learner supplies the appropriate amount of information in reporting or describing some idea, statement, or action. In the Jakobovits and Gordon scheme, the two poles for rating "amount of information related" are "very little" and "all of it." In his study, however, Levenston points out that if anything, some foreign students were verbose in response to the situations he gave them. In other words, they tended to say more than the native would. For example, let us take the following situation:

> You buy some milk, but when you get home you find that it is sour. You take it back to the store and speak to the manager.

According to Levenston (1975), native speakers would say, "I bought this milk here this afternoon, and it's sour." Thus the natives were leaving it up to the manager to suggest an exchange, whereas the foreign learners added on more information by asking directly for the exchange as well. Thus "amount of information related" is assessed in the present scale in terms of appropriateness: (1) not appropriate to (5) appropriate.

I was originally going to add to Levenston's two dimensions, *form* and *content*, a third dimension *fluency*, since Savignon included such a category. But first of all, she defined "verbal fluency" in terms of the effort which learners make to speak (how much they attempt to communicate), an approach which would have verbal fluency overlap with "amount of information related" (scale 6 under "content"). And second, "fluency" is not easy to assess, even impressionistically. For example, there are problems associated with criteria such as "speed" or "ease of speech." As Kato (1977) points out, people differ in terms of speech rate even in their native language, and speaking "easily" does not necessarily mean speaking appropriately. In going back over transcripts of oral exams, Kato found that in reality, certain nonnative students that he and others had marked as more fluent than other students were actually not as good at selecting appropriate vocabulary, nor at grammatical control. In fact, the very hesitation phenomena (e.g., pauses filled with "er" or "uh") that make a foreign speaker's speech seem broken may really be signs that the person is searching for the appropriate lexical item or grammatical structure.

Researchers are now suggesting that any simplified rating scales of fluency are of dubious value, since natives may perform more poorly than nonnatives in that nonnatives are making a conscientious effort to speak without obvious hesitation, to use longer sentences, use an accelerated tempo, etc. (Sajavaara and Lehtonen 1978). It is even suggested that it may be valuable to teach students how to be *disfluent,* so that they can sound more native-like. Lehtonen (1978) puts it as follows:

> To be fluent in the right way, one has to know how to hesitate, how to be silent, how to self-correct, how to interrupt and how to complete one's expression. According to this definition of fluency, one must speak in a way that is expected by the linguistic community and that represents normal, acceptable and relaxed linguistic behavior. Testing of this quality of speech is not possible by means of any instrumental method. (p. 12)

Thus "fluency" is being excluded from the current rating scale.

Preliminary application of this Rating Scale for Pragmatic Speaking has indicated that it is possible to distinguish the different rating categories from one another, and that the distinction between form and content appears to be empirically viable.[12] As is true with rating scales, no matter how rigorously pretested, it will ultimately be up to the classroom teacher to make reliable use of the scales across students and with the same student over time; and this task of establishing reliability (getting an accurate assessment) will probably call for some practice on the teacher's part. It has been suggested that a rigorous, reliable rating of listening comprehension, pronunciation, grammar, fluency, and overall speaking proficiency required a minimum of two judges (regardless of whether they were receiving training in linguistics) (Mullen 1977). Here again, in the classroom, the teacher does not usually have the luxury of calling in another judge. In some settings, fellow students could act as judges, as described above with respect to testing pronunciation and writing skills. Or it could simply be clear from the outset that the ratings are impressionistic and intended as suggestive of the relative strengths and weaknesses of each learner.

There is also a problem of validity. Students might not speak in class the way they actually would if performing in the real world. They may be using inappropriate constructions precisely because they feel these are to be used in the classroom. The teacher would have to make it clear to the students that they are to sound native -like. The students should, in fact, be aware of just what each rating scale is rating, and should try their best to throw themselves into the role that they are playing in the dialog. This extra motivation on the part of the student to perfom in as native -like a way as possible results in integrative test-response data that are more pragmatic in nature. Thus the teacher assumes the role of external motivator such that the students themselves become motivated to engage in such a dialog.

It is important to point out that not all the categories of this Rating Scale for Pragmatic Speaking may be relevant for rating a given speech situation. For example "accuracy of information" pertains to reporting, retelling, or describing something and so may not apply to a variety of dialogs—unless, for example, one or another participant is given information to report.

Furthermore, it is important to overlook grammatical problems as much as possible in rating pragmatic speaking, although linguistic criteria may inadvertently influence a rater's judgment (Schulz and Bartz 1975). Inappropriate choice of vocabulary should also be overlooked in scoring *if* it does not interfere with the communication of the information (i.e., an error for which the appropriate word is obvious). It could be argued, as Canale and Swain (1979) do, that a measure of functional language ability or communicative competence must include measurement of grammatical competence as well. I would still encourage the teacher to attempt to exclude grammatical problems from consideration in initial efforts at rating pragmatic speaking ability. This dimension can easily be added once the other dimensions have been rated.

Classroom procedures for rating

Rating activities are to be performed in the classroom during regular class sessions. For example, pairs of students can take turns indulging in short (10 to 15 minute) conversations. If possible, students should converse with a native speaker aside from the teacher in order to simulate a typical nonclassroom situation (in environments where learners come in regular contact with native speakers). Learner-to-learner dialogs (referred to as "interlanguage talk"; see Krashen 1978) are probably different from learner-to-native speaker dialogs in certain characteristic ways. Learners may sound more native-like when addressing a native speaker expressly because the demands are greater, and therefore their motivation is enhanced. Clearly learners will differ in this respect.

The teacher may wish to make an audiotape or even a videotape (if equipment is available) simply to verify one or more aspects of the ratings after the conversation is over, but the conversation need not be taped. Scoring should be conducted by and large while the students are speaking. Obviously, this means that the teacher will have to practice applying the ratings. Such a classroom exercise and rating scale could be used even at the beginning levels of language learning. Scores might be expected to be higher for students taking a course which, say, stresses conversation and especially the teaching of functional language use—appropriate speech acts for given discourse situations.

The sample dialog below is intended to clarify the procedures for scoring.

A sample dialog

In the sample dialog below, the speakers are not intended to represent any particular native-language group. It should be pointed out that in this case, both participants in the dialog are learners of the target language, and thus both would get a score for their performance.

* * * * * *

Simulated Conversation between Two Students of English

Given the following situation: A boy (George) calls a girl (Julie) for a date. He met her at a party the previous week. He has bought two tickets to a rock concert, and really wants to take her out. She's not interested in him at all.

(The phone rings.)
1. *Julie*: Hello.
2. *George*: Who's this?
3. *Julie*: Who are you?
4. *George*: This George. I could speak to Julie?
5. *Julie*: This is Julie.
6. *George*: Oh, Julie, remember we meet last week at Bill party. How are you?
7. *Julie*: O.K. Very busy with exams now. For anything I have no time.
8. *George*: Well, this what I want to talk you. I bought cards to rock concert Wednesday night. It will be for me big pleasure if you can have time to go with me the concert that I have bought the cards for it.
9. *Julie*: Even I really want to, I take exam Thursday and I have to learn first.

10. *George*: You study the day, you have still the night to go. It's well a break from study.
11. *Julie*: I'm nervous before exam and because of this I will not enjoy in the concert. And also best directly before the test I study.
12. *George*: O.K. Maybe I buy cards for next week?
13. *Julie*: It's too far ahead for plan. I maybe not in town.
14. *George*: O.K. Well, I give a call next week.
15. *Julie*: If you want to call, I will be really very busy.
16. *George*: It seem you don't like me and don't want to go out with me, right?
17. *Julie*: No, I don't. And thanks for calling.
18. *George*: It's not any trouble. Goodbye.

* * * * * *

Now let us rate the conversation according to the Rating Scale for Pragmatic Speaking:

Form: 1. *Naturalness of Discourse*—The question is whether the speakers selected and ordered their discourse elements appropriately. George's move to identify the person answering the phone first, through "Who's this?" appears to violate a rule about how people establish who is who on the phone. In an English-mother-tongue country, at least in the United States, the person calling someone at his home might be expected to identify himself first, before the person being called. (Procedures in a business office may be different.) Let us assume that in George's country of origin, the person being called at home is expected to identify himself first. George might then be rated a 3 on this subscale. Although he initiates the call unnaturally, he handles the speech acts of requesting and persuading rather well. Julie has a good sense of discourse rules. She corrects what she perceives as George's breaking of a conversation in (2) "Who's this?" by asking in (3) "Who are you?" She then displays facility with other speech acts, namely, refusing and making excuses. If we ignore the many grammatical errors and the several lexical errors (which is not so easy to do), we are able to award her a 5 in naturalness of discourse.

2. *Style of Expression*—George has several stylistic problems. For example, he says in (8), "Will you go with me?" instead of "I thought you might like to go with me," or "Would you be able to go with me?" Then he says in (18), "It is not any trouble," instead of "Oh, that's O.K." or "Don't mention it." He might be rated as 4. Julie's style is also somewhat nonnative-like. In (17), a native would say something

like, "No, I guess I don't" or "Maybe I don't," in order to soften the blow rather than "No, I don't." She might also be rated 4.[13]

3. *Clarity of Expression*— Most of the discourse is clear, but there are some unclear utterances. For example, take George's utterance (10), "You study the day, you have still the night to go. It's well a break from study." It may take a little interpreting for the average native listener to realize what his point is. Julie has even more unclear utterances: (7) "For anything I have no time." (9) "Even I really want to, I take exam Thursday and I have to learn first." (11) "And also best directly before the test I study." (15) "If you want to call, I will be really very busy." I would score George as 4 and Julie as 3 on clarity.

Content: 4. *Suitability*— This category is based on rather circumscribed conventions for what is socially acceptable in a given exchange. In the above dialog, there is at least one remark that may not be considered acceptable with respect to content. In (16), George says, "It seem you don't like me and don't want go out with me, right?" In the United States, at least, a native speaker might be thinking such content, but he would probably not say it directly like this. He may say, "Well, I guess I won't try again," so as to imply that he is aware that the girl does not want to go out with him. Thus, rating of content really concerns distinguishing messages which are communicated directly by natives from those which are perhaps thought but not delivered verbally in the conversation.

In rating George and Julie, we may decide to give George a 3, as an average of both suitable and unsuitable content. Julie would get a 5 because her sense of content seems suitable throughout the conversation.

5. *Accuracy of Information*— This category does not apply because the speakers are not being called upon to report or describe ideas, statements, or actions.

6. *Amount of Information Related*— As noted above, learners of a language may sound verbose in their efforts to communicate information. This verbosity may result from a conscious effort to avoid structures that they do not know well or simply from a desire to be sure to get their message across. In (8), George could simply have asked Julie, "Could you go with me?" Instead, his utterance ("It will be for me big pleasure if . . .") is elaborate and repetitive. I would rate him a 3 for this category, suggesting that he is not relating the appropriate amount of information. Julie would get a 5 in that her utterances seem to include the appropriate amount of information.

In sum, the following are the scores for George and Julie by category:

Form	George	Julie
Naturalness of discourse	3	5
Style of expression	4	4
Clarity of expression	4	3
Content		
Suitability	3	5
Accuracy of information	—	—
Amount of information related	3	5
	17	22

The scoring is best done by dividing total number of points by total number of scales actually used in a given analysis. Thus George would receive a score of 17 of a possible 25 points (5 categories, 5 points per category) = 68 percent, and Julie would get a score of 22/25 = 88 per cent.

There is no doubt that an exercise like this raises more questions than it can answer. First, we have to remember that in this exercise we are assessing spoken dialog from a written text. In actual dialogs, inappropriate phonological features (segmental and suprasegmental) often interfere with comprehension at a basic, encoding level. Second, native speakers vary in their tolerance for nonnative features. It may well be that owing to training and experience, teachers will be better able to reconstruct in their own minds what students meant to say when they produced an unclear utterance. Thus it may be difficult for the teacher to find genuinely unclear utterances that would affect the student's rating under "clarity of expression."

Furthermore, is it fair to compare nonnatives with some sort of native model? Which native model should you use—i.e., that of a peer, with the same educational background, assuming the same role, etc.? The research by Sajavaara and Lehtonen (1978) on nonnatives being rated more fluent than natives may pertain to certain rating scales on this suggested instrument as well (e.g., on sounding native-like in style of expression). The literature has raised the issue of communicative competence/pragmatic speaking as a *measurable* phenomenon. This example, I believe, points up the difficulties in actual measurement.

Let us take the suitability of content of what Julie said to George, for example. What if she had started telling George that she did not want to go out with him because he was ugly looking, acted obnoxiously, and reminded her of an old boyfriend she had had and whom she came to hate? Might not this content be acceptable under certain circumstances—e.g., if said in rage or in jest?

The reader will also notice that the number of points to be awarded within a given category is suggested somewhat tentatively. This is because there are as yet no clear-cut guidelines as to what constitutes, say, a 4 in "naturalness of discourse." Perhaps a rule of thumb is that a 2 means more unnatural than natural, a 3 means somewhere in the middle between unnatural and natural, a 4 means more natural than unnatural, and so forth. But how is the middle rating of 3 established? One means of determining rating is by the frequency with which unnatural discourse forms occur. For example, if only two out of four speech acts are performed naturally, the speaker gets a 3. However, teachers may feel that the unnaturalness of a single speech act is great enough to prompt them to give the speaker a rating of 3.

My hunch is that even though this type of rating scale is in need of more extensive empirical validation it is less threatening, and hopefully more instructional, to the students involved than is the traditional set of scales based on grammatical accuracy, pronunciation, and the like. It may also help students to get a better idea of what it means to gain pragmatic control of the language. It is encouraging to note that increasing efforts are being made to test the ability to perform various speech acts in a foreign language. For example, there apparently are large-scale projects underway aimed specifically at testing students through their participation in dialogs, wherein situation, roles, speech acts to be performed, and informational aspects to be dealt with are all specified at the outset (see, for instance, Roos-Wijgh 1978).

In Short

This chapter has laid out options for using three of the more pragmatic types of integrative tests, namely, cloze, dictation, and speaking. Cloze is a versatile measure in terms of what it tests directly (namely, ability to read and write cohesive English) and indirectly (namely, speaking ability and listening). Yet this treatment has also tried to include discussion of problems with cloze, such as the need to use discretionary judgment in determining which words to delete (rather than simply random deletion) and problems in scoring.

Dictation is offered as a more focused, structured activity than cloze, but also as a technique which, if used pragmatically (i.e., larger chunks of information, presented at a normal pace, etc.), can tap a student's ability to understand spoken language in an integrative, global fashion.

Finally, the section on pragmatic speaking offers a composite system for rating speaking *without* rating for many of the aspects usually rated for, such as grammar, pronunciation, and intonation. Then a simulated dialog is presented and rated, for purposes of discussion.

Hopefully, this chapter has raised issues that will influence a given teacher's decision as to whether to use one or another of these tests in some form or fashion in the classroom.

Notes

1. "Second-language spew" refers to word-association data that are analyzed so as to produce a response hierarchy characteristic of that language/culture group (Jakobovits 1970).

2. In the clozentropy scoring method (Darnell 1968), the respondent's choice for a given blank is assigned a weighted score corresponding to the natural logarithm of the number of native speakers who selected that choice when they were given the same cloze in a previous testing session.

3. This was the procedure adopted for use with university-level cloze tests of English achievement at the Hebrew University of Jerusalem, 1977-1978.

4. Another modification consists of supplying all the deleted words in random order after the passage. Then the student is to choose items by the process of elimination.

5. Recent research found that a cloze test using this type of acceptable-word scoring actually proved more reliable than a cloze scored on an exact-word basis (Rand 1978).

6. *Syntactic acceptability*: 4 = acceptable, 3 = acceptable at the sentence level but not at the discourse level, 2 = acceptable only with a subsequent portion of the sentence, 1 = acceptable only with a preceding part of the sentence, 0 = unacceptable. *Semantic acceptability*: 6 = acceptable, 5 = acceptable at the passage level ignoring minor syntactic error, 4 = acceptable at the sentence level but not at the discourse level, 3 = acceptable at the sentence level ignoring minor syntactic error, 2 = acceptable only with the subsequent part of sentence, 1 = acceptable only with the preceding portion of sentence, 0 = totally unacceptable. *Semantic change* (if rated 6 for semantic acceptability): 3 = no change, 2 = minor change in meaning of sentence, connotation, 1 = major change—conveys author's meaning but is "unusual" or "nonnative."

7. My thanks go to Nelson Berkoff, English as a Foreign Language Department, Hebrew University, for permitting me to use his item analysis of the data.

8. Of course, if spelling *is* a goal of instruction, it should be scored—perhaps separately.

9.   Descriptions of some of the features of fast speech in American English are readily available (e.g., Bowen 1975). A teacher may purposely wish to include some of these features in a pragmatic dictation.

10.   Pilot testing consists of trying out the test on a group of students similar to those for whom the test is intended. Then results are analyzed, and modifications are made according to the findings. The designation of one-third point to each error and thus a maximum of 45 points was, despite the pilot testing, an arbitrary decision, not based on statistical rigor. Of course, our concern here is for scoring procedures that teachers could use easily.

11.   The authors prefer the term "transactional competence" to "communicative competence" in that "communicative" suggests the transmission of information, whereas the ordinary uses of language are chiefly oriented to "the structured display of rituals in the form of transactional moves and replies" (Jakobovits and Gordon 1974, p. 249).

12.   I obtained evidence from a group of 25 student teachers that the six scales presented in this instrument can be distinguished from one another—i.e., that they do, in fact, assess different phenomena. It would still be useful to obtain formal intra-rater and inner-rater reliability data.

A colleague and I have also been researching another approach to assessing pragmatic speaking ability or "sociocultural competence," using Canale and Swain's (1979) model of communicative competence—i.e., grammatical competence, discourse competence (cohesion and coherence), sociocultural competence (culture and style), and communication strategies. So far we have just tested ability to apologize in a foreign language, using native speakers of the native and foreign languages for control purposes. For more on this approach, see Cohen and Olshtain 1980.

13.   We note that "style of expression" actually involves the ability to choose from among several grammatically acceptable forms the one that reflects the appropriate degree of deference, politeness, formality, or whatever, for the given context.

Chapter 6
Taking Stock

The intent of this volume was not to present a lengthy treatise on language testing. Rather, the intent was to focus on a limited number of topics. The initial aim was to write a testing book around the edges of other testing books—i.e., covering topics not covered in much depth elsewhere. The reader must be the judge as to whether this goal has been achieved.

Another key focus was on the needs of the classroom teacher on a daily basis. If a classroom teacher can read the preceding five chapters and come away with some practical ideas for use in the classroom, the book will have met one of its major objectives.

At first, I thought that I would avoid referring to research literature in that the emphasis was on practical suggestions. But as I started writing, I realized how prescriptive it would sound if I suggested that teachers do X or Y without giving a rationale. Hence there are references to research. My personal view is that the classroom teacher can help in the research effort. Take, for instance, the issue of whether there is a "practice effect" associated with the cloze test. The classroom teacher could investigate whether performance on cloze does, in fact, improve with training and exposure to such tests.

A question that kept going through my mind as I was writing this book was, "To what extent does a second-language syllabus stimulate the development of tests to match it, to what extent do tests themselves stimulate a particular line of teaching, and to what extent is the influence two-way?" In his book on notional syllabuses, for example, Wilkins (1976) states that "it is important that while some people are experimenting with the notional syllabus as such, others should be attempting to develop the new testing techniques that should, ideally, accompany it" (p. 82). Over the years, a negative stigma has always been attached to "teaching to the test." But if a test really reflects the essence of a syllabus, and especially if this syllabus emphasizes skill-using or communicative ability, there is every reason to expect the relationship between teaching and testing to be close, and to be two-way. A cloze test, for example, may itself stimulate types of classroom activities aimed at determining whether students have understood a passage. In fact, at times there may be little ostensible difference to the outside observer between a learning exercise and a testing exercise.

I suppose that the issue is one of degree. When a particular testing format on, say, a comprehensive matriculation exam dictates the teaching procedures for one or more courses, there is an imbalance in need of redress. At a far less comprehensive level, a clever testing procedure may contribute one or more fresh ideas concerning how to go about teaching language and stimulating language learning, and such a spin-off, of course, would be all for the better.

There is probably no ideal point at which to cease revising the manuscript of a book of this kind before publishing it. In some ways, the field of testing is moving so fast that even the focal issues "around the edges" change from one day to the next. Hopefully, this book has touched on issues that are, in fact, in fashion. The book also noted from time to time the swing of the pendulum back toward previous approaches to testing, however much enlightened these approaches may now be, given the new types of knowledge that have accrued in the interim period. In fact, it may not ultimately matter so much which type of items or tests we use, but rather what we *know* about these tests before we even give them, what we learn about how the students produce answers to these tests, and what we do about evaluating these answers. A teacher who can feel comfortable in these areas has nothing to fear about quizzing or testing students. In fact, such activities can even be seen as a welcome and stimulating challenge.

Glossary

achievement testing: a measure of what has been learned from what was taught in a particular course or series of courses.

alternate-response format: an item-response format whereby one of two alternatives is the right answer, i.e., true/false, correct/incorrect, yes/no, same/different, 1 or 2.

appositive phrase: typically one of two phrases which is a constituent at the same level as the other one (i.e., coordinated) and which overlaps or is identical to the second in terms of what it refers to, e.g., "Harvey, *our new neighbor,* bought a turtle."

cloze: a test procedure (q.v.) which elicits the completion of blanks deleted from a text; the word "cloze" was coined in reference to the notion of psychological "closure."

cognitive style: the learner's predisposition to adopt certain patterns of intellectual functioning, such as with regard to field dependence (q.v.), interference (q.v.), and overgeneralization (q.v.).

cohesion: relations of meaning that exist within a text and that define it as a text; these relations are both grammatical (e.g., through reference (q.v.)) and lexical.

collocation: a regular pattern of co-occurrence in which lexical items may be found in the same immediate environment, e.g., of non-idiomatic collocation: "quite pregnant"; idiomatic collocation: "to take a break."

Community Language Learning: a method of learning a target language in a small group whereby the teacher is a counselor and the learner is a client who initiates responses which are, in the first stages of learning, translated by the counselor, and in turn repeated by learners as they direct their comments or ideas to someone in the group.

contextual guesser: a second-language reader who keeps the story or theme in mind while reading, checks to see if words make sense in context, and does not give up.

contextual paraphrase: a phrase which is synonymous with another phrase in a given text, e.g.,

"On the day before   the voting took place   ... there was
                                        A
much politicking before   the ballots were cast   ."
                                        B

B is a contextual paraphrase of A.

contrastive analysis: a comparison of forms in the native language and in the target language; aimed at describing differences and similarities in forms, their functions, and relative frequency in their respective languages.

copula: the verb "to be" when used as a link between the subject and the predicate noun or adjective, e.g., "She *is* a lawyer." "He *is* nice."

coreference: when two expressions have the same reference, e.g., "Daniel taught *himself*." "When she got home, Naomi took a bath"—only if "she" refers to Naomi and not to someone else.

criterion-referenced testing: an approach to quizzing or testing which evaluates individual performance in terms of some predetermined criterion for success at performing some behavior with some result under certain conditions and judged by certain standards, e.g., writing a friendly letter in the target language (the behavior), consisting of 50 words or more (the result), within 10 minutes (the condition), with no more than three morphological errors (the standard).

cross-association errors: student errors resulting when a teacher or textbook presents two words or constructions too close together and/or not thoroughly enough, such that the learner has not learned the first well enough to distinguish it correctly from the second.

decoding ability: the ability to derive meaning from oral or written input.

direct test: a test that samples directly from the behavior being evaluated, e.g., students are tested on their ability to give a talk in class— a direct measure of one type of speaking behavior.

discrete-point testing: testing of one point at a time; i.e., only one element (e.g., negative singular past auxiliary "didn't") from one component of language (e.g., syntax) is assessed in one skill (reading), a receptive skill (q.v.).

distinctive elements of a test or quiz: the individual features that are combined in producing tests or quizzes, including the item-stimulus format (q.v.), the item-response format (q.v.), and the item type (q.v.).

distractor: an alternate-response choice which is intended to attract students who do not know the right answer.

dominant language: the language that an individual is strongest in at a given moment; it may be the native language (q.v.) or another language.

ellipsis: the deletion of something which is considered to be understood from the context; it is presupposed that some preceding item serves as the source of the missing information; e.g., "Joan brought some roses, and Jill some mushrooms" (i.e., Jill brought mushrooms).

encoding ability: the ability to produce oral or written output.

face validity: whether the test, on the fact of it, *appears* to measure what it claims to measure.

field dependence: distraction from elements that are in the immediate environment but irrelevant to the language processing being called for, e.g., producing an utterance like, "The list of people *are* on the table" because the object of the preposition, "people," distracted the speaker away from the appropriate singular form to agree with "list."

field independence: the ability to break up an organized visual field and to keep a part of it separate from that field. (*Note*: general psychological definition, not specifically related to language learning.)

fixed response: the respondent is to make choices from among existing alternatives (such as with alternate, multiple-choice, or matching-response formats).

foreign-language testing: testing skills in a target language that is not used widely in the community, e.g., teaching English in Israel.

free response: respondents have the liberty to say or write what they choose, usually within certain parameters.

functional language ability: the ability to use target language knowledge in natural or naturalistic communicative situations (q.v.).

homophony: equivalence in sound between words, but a difference in the written form, origin, and meaning, e.g., "to," "too," "two,"; "bare," "bear."

indirect test: a test that is contrived and/or different from the situation of interest; e.g., students are given a short-answer grammar test as an indirect measure of their actual grammatical performance in normal classroom routines or out of class.

integrative testing: testing two or more points together, usually implying the testing of a number of such points at once (*see* testing point).

interference: the production of incorrect target-language forms through the influence of forms in the native language; also referred to as "negative transfer" (q.v.).

interrater reliability: a measure of the degree to which two or more raters agree in their ratings on some behavior assessed in one or more subjects.

introspective account: students' descriptions of the process or strategies they are using to accomplish some task (e.g., complete a test item), obtained at the moment the process is taking place.

item analysis: looking at the results of a test in terms of item difficulty (q.v.) and item discrimination (q.v.).

item difficulty: the proportion of correct responses to total responses on a test item, e.g., if 20 out of 30 students get an item right, the item difficulty is 66 percent (20/30).

item discrimination: how well an item distinguishes better students from poorer ones. For example, if the upper third of the students get the item correct and the lower two-thirds generally get it wrong, the item is a good discriminator between these two groups.

item-response format: the format which the student is to use in order to respond to an item stimulus; the response may make use of the oral, written, or nonverbal medium, or some combination of these.

item-stimulus format: the format for eliciting data on a test item or procedure; the item stimulus may make use of the oral, written, or nonverbal medium, or some combination of these.

item type: the product of combining an item stimulus with an item response; e.g., one item type could consist of a reading passage followed by statements about it (item stimulus) with true/false alongside each statement (item response).

language aptitude: basic ability to learn a new language, including verbal intelligence, auditory and visual memory span, sound-symbol associative skill, and skill at grammatical analysis.

linguistic competence: the breadth of knowledge that the learner has regarding the linguistic elements of the language—pronunciation, vocabulary, and structure.

macro-context: the larger context within which a form is found—i.e., in written texts, a sentence, paragraph, section, or passage as a whole.

mean score: the average score for a given group of students, obtained by adding all the individual scores and the dividing by the total number of scores.

median interval: the interval which includes the point below and above which 50 percent of the scores occur.

micro-context: the immediate context of a form—i.e., the word, words, or phrase that the deleted word is immediately associated with. In the following example, the micro-context for "knowing" is italicized: *"without quite* knowing *why."*

minimal pair: two words sounding alike in all but one feature, e.g., "heating"–"hitting." In this case, the feature is the first vowel /i/ vs. /ɪ/.

miscue analysis: analysis of errors in oral reading, such as omission, substitution, word insertion, and mispronunciation; the analysis also checks for dialect forms, difficulty with word parts, and repetition to correct an error in reading.

morpheme: a minimal unit of speech that is recurrent and meaningful. It may be a word or part of a word, e.g., the word *un-friend-ly* has three morphemes, *sit-s* has two.

native language: the first language acquired, i.e., that language acquired as a mother tongue; sometimes there may be more than one "native" language.

naturalistic communicative situation: a staged situation, usually in a classroom, which is intended to simulate natural communication removed from the intervention of an instructor.

negative transfer: the production of incorrect target-language forms through the influence of forms in the native language; also referred to as "interference." For example, "This is the boy that I spoke about *him,"* because in the native language, the subordinate clause includes the equivalent of the object pronoun "him."

norms: an empirically derived distribution of scores on a test, which provides reference data for appropriate groups of examinees; e.g., students' results on the Test of English as a Foreign Language (TOEFL) are reported with reference to norms so that students can see where they stand in comparison with the general population of foreign students.

overgeneralization: producing an incorrect target-language form out of false analogy to another form within the target language, e.g., "He didn't *found* it," out of analogy to "He found it."

paraphrase: saying the same thing or roughly the same thing in different words and/or using different syntactic structures, e.g., "The accident was caused by Tom's negligence."/"Tom's negligence caused the accident."/"Tom's carelessness brought about the accident."

percentile rank: a number indicating the percent of individuals within the specific norm group (cf. *norms*) that scored lower than the raw score (q.v.) of a given student.

phonemes: the smallest segments of sound that can be distinguished by their contrast within words. For example, in the word "heat," there are three phonemes, /h/, /i/, and /t/; the word "hot" has the same first and third phoneme, while the second phoneme /a/ is different and changes the meaning of the word. These words, "hit" and "hot," are therefore minimal pairs (q.v.).

pragmatic testing: testing of the ability to use the target language in simulated or actual communicative contexts.

prepackaged material: forms which have been acquired without being fully analyzed, if at all, e.g., "I don't wanna eat this; I don't *wanna* that also."

presystematic stage: learners are unaware of the existence of a particular system or rule in the target language; they may produce a correct form occasionally, but the forms are mostly wrong and learners do not know how to correct them.

productive skills: skills which call for producing output, either oral (through speaking) or written (through writing).

proficiency test: a measure of the linguistic knowledge that students have in a language and/or their ability to apply this knowledge functionally.

quiz: a short measure of class material, possibly informal in nature; e.g., a quiz may just check for ability to use 10 target-language words in a sentence.

raw score: the score obtained directly as a result of tallying up all the items answered correctly on a test.

receptive skills: skills which call for processing input—either aural (through listening) or written (through reading).

reference: relates to items in a language (often pronouns) which acquire their semantic interpretation through their relationship to something else (appearing earlier in the text or utterance, later, or not at all), e.g., "Three blind mice. See how *they* run."

register: a language variety usually characterized by a certain level of formality (e.g., formal, casual, intimate), possibly by identification with a certain social group (e.g., politicians, taxi drivers), or medium (e.g., the spoken register of prisoners, the written register of lawyers).

reliability: the accuracy with which an item or test is measuring what it is measuring, i.e., the likelihood that the obtained result would be replicated if the item or test were given again to the same students.

retrospective account: students' attempt to recollect the process by which they accomplished some task (e.g., completed a test item) at some point in the past (five minutes earlier, an hour earlier, the day before, etc.).

scoring of test: determining the number of points that each item or procedure is to receive, and then the value or weighting of these points with respect to the total test or quiz.

second-language testing: testing skills in a target language that is used widely in the community, e.g., teaching English in the United States.

Silent Way: a method of learning a target language wherein the students do 90 percent or more of the talking from the very start, while the teacher remains almost completely silent; speech is accompanied by appropriate action, generally the manipulation of a set of rods.

skill-getting activities: activities aimed at developing linguistic competence—i.e., a perception of language categories, functions, and the rules relating the two; practice in producing sound segments and in formulating communication.

skill-using activities: activities aimed at developing functional language ability—i.e., an ability to perform in natural or naturalistic communicative situations (q.v.).

standardized test: a measure that has been piloted (usually on a large sample, representing different types of respondents) and for which interpretive data, such as norms (q.v.), reliability (q.v.), and validity (q.v.) coefficients have been provided.

stem: the initial part of an item—either a partial sentence to be completed, a question, or several statements leading to a question or an incomplete phrase.

structured response: respondents are to contribute some of their own input to the answer (e.g., ordering of elements, identifying, or completion).

syntagmatic relationship: a relationship between two or more words by virtue of their syntactic combination in a phrase; e.g., in the expression "the busy pigeon," the adjective "busy" is syntagmatically related to the definite article "the" and the noun "pigeon."

target language: the language that is being acquired as a second or foreign language.

test: a formal measure of skill, announced in advance and requiring a substantial amount of time to complete (i.e., an hour or more). For example, a test might include a reading passage with questions, a grammar section, and a series of words to use in sentences.

tested response behavior: the differential emphasis (or emphases) that the item or procedure gives to the following aspects of responding—quantity of response, accuracy, and speed.

testing objective: the explicit intent of an item or procedure, such as to test for a particular discrete point (q.v.).

testing point: any feature or form that a given item elicits, including both points intended to be tested by the item as well as the full range of points actually elicited by a given item (with or without the teacher's awareness).

test item: one entry or question on a test or quiz, e.g., of an item: "Write out a sentence using the word 'salubrious.' "

test procedure: a sizable task elicited on a test or quiz, e.g., of a procedure: "Write several paragraphs summarizing the movie that you just saw."

validity: the extent to which a test *actually* measures what it purports to measure (in contrast to *face* validity, q.v.).

weighting of items: assigning point scores to items and procedures on a quiz or test; items may all be weighted equally (i.e., fixed-interval weighting) or may be weighted differently according to their importance or difficulty relative to other items on the test.

References

Aighes, Brenda, et al. *Progress Report on the BBN Group.* University of Illinois at Urbana/ Champaign & Bolt Beranek and Newman, 50 Moulton St., Cambridge, Mass. 02138. BBN Report No. 3720, prepared for National Institute of Education, 1977.

Aitken, Kenneth F. "Using Cloze Procedure as an Overall Language Proficiency Test." *TESOL Quarterly,* 1977, *11* (1), 59–67.

Alderson, John Charles. "The Use of Cloze Procedure with Native and Non-Native Speakers of English." Ph.D. Dissertation, University of Edinburgh, 1978.

Allen, Edward D. "Miscue Analysis: A New Tool for Diagnosing Oral Reading Proficiency in Foreign Languages." *Foreign Language Annals,* 1976, *9* (6), 563–567.

Allen, Edward D. and Valette, Rebecca A. *Classroom Techniques: Foreign Languages and English as a Second Language.* New York: Harcourt Brace Jovanovich, 1977.

Allwright, Richard. "Problems in the Study of Language Teachers' Treatment of Learner Errors." In M. K. Burt and H. D. Dulay, eds. *On TESOL '75. New Directions in Second Language Learning, Teaching and Bilingual Education,* Washington, D.C.: TESOL, 1975, 96–109.

Alpert R. and Haber, R. N. "Anxiety in Academic Achievement Situations." *Journal of Abnormal and Social Psychology,* 1960, *61,* 207–215.

Anderson, Jonathan. *Psycholinguistic Experiments in Foreign Language Testing.* St. Lucia, Queensland, Australia: University of Queensland Press, 1976.

Berkoff, Nelson A. "A Diagnostic Use of Cloze Testing." *English Teachers' Journal (Israel),* 1976, *16,* 42–50.

Bormuth, John R. "Comparable Cloze and Multiple-Choice Comprehension Test Scores." *Journal of Reading,* 1967, *10,* 291–299.

Bormuth, John R. *On the Theory of Achievement Test Items.* Chicago: University of Chicago Press, 1970.

Bowen, J. Donald. "A Tentative Measure of the Relative Control of English and Amharic by Eleventh-Grade Ethiopian Students." *Workpapers in Teaching English as a Second Language,* 1969, *2,* University of California, Los Angeles, 69–89.

Bowen, J. Donald. "Contextualizing Pronunciation Practice in the ESOL Classroom." *TESOL Quarterly,* 1972, *6* (1), 83–94.

Bowen, J. Donald. *Patterns of English Pronunciation.* Rowley, Mass.: Newbury House, 1975.

Bowen, J. Donald. "Practice Effect in English Proficiency Testing." In H.D. Brown, C.A. Yorio, and R.H. Crymes, eds. *On TESOL '77. Teaching and Learning English as a Second Language: Trends in Research and Practice.* Washington, D.C.: TESOL, 1977, 295–308.

Brière, Eugène J. "Testing the Control of Parts of Speech in FL Compositions." *Language Learning,* 1964, *14* (1), 1–9.

Brière, Eugene J. "Phonological Testing Reconsidered." *Language Learning,* 1967, *17* (3, 4), 163–171.

Brière, Eugène J., Clausing, Gerhard, Senko, Donna, and Purcell, Edward. "A Look at Cloze Testing across Languages and Levels." *Modern Language Journal,* 1978, *62* (1–2), 23–26.

Brooks, Nelson. "Making Your Own Language Tests." In M.R. Donoghue, ed. *Foreign Languages and the Schools: A Book of Readings.* Dubuque, Iowa: Wm. C. Brown Co., 1967, 285–302.

Buck, Catherine. "Miscues of Non-Native Speakers of English." In K.S. Goodman, ed. *Miscue Analysis: Applications to Reading Instruction.* Urbana, Ill.: National Council of Teachers of English, 1973, 91–96.

Burt, Marina K. and Kiparsky, Carol. *The Gooficon: A Repair Manual for English.* Rowley, Mass.: Newbury House, 1972.

Burt, Marina K., Dulay, Heidi C., and Hernández-Chavez, Eduardo. *The Bilingual Syntax Measure.* New York: Harcourt Brace Jovanovich, 1975.

Canale, Michael and Swain, Merrill. "Theoretical Bases of Communicative Approaches to Second Language Teaching and Testing." *Applied Linguistics,* 1980, *1* (1) 1–47.

Candlin, Christopher N, Kirkwood, J. M., and Moore, H. M. "Study Skills in English: Theoretical Issues and Practical Problems." In R. MacKay and A. Mountford, eds. *English for Specified Purposes.* London: Longman, 1978, 190–219.

Carroll, John B. "The Psychology of Language Testing." In A. Davies, ed. *Language Testing Symposium: A Psycholinguistic Approach.* London: Oxford University Press, 1968, 46–69.

Carroll, John B. "Defining Language Comprehension: Some Speculations." In Roy B. Freedle and John B. Carroll, eds. *Language Comprehension and the Acquisition of Knowledge.* Washington, D.C.: V.H. Winston, 1972, 1–29.

Carroll, John B. "Foreign Language Testing: Will the Persistent Problems Persist?" In M.C. O'Brien, ed. *Testing in Second Language Teaching: New Dimensions.* Ireland: ATESOL, Dublin University Press, 1973, 6–17.

Carroll, J. B., Carton, A. S., and Wilds, C. P. "An Investigation of 'Cloze' Items in the Measurement of Achievement in Foreign Languages." College Entrance Examination Board Research and Development Report, Laboratory for Research in Instruction, Harvard University, Cambridge, Mass., 1959.

Celce-Murcia, Marianne. "Report of an Informal Classroom Experiment on Speed-writing with a Suggestion for Further Research." *Workpapers in Teaching English as a Second Language,* 1974, *8,* 63–69.

Chastain, Kenneth. *Developing Second Language Skills: Theory to Practice.* 2d ed., Chicago: Rand McNalley, 1976.

Chihara, Tetsuro, Oller, John, Weaver, Kelley, and Chávez-Oller, Mary Anne. "Are Cloze Items Sensitive to Constraints across Sentences?" *Language Learning,* 1977, *27* (1), 63–73.

Clark, John L. D. *Foreign Language Testing: Theory and Practice.* Philadelphia: The Center for Curriculum Development, 1972.

Clark, John L. D. *The Performance of Native Speakers of English on the Test of English as a Foreign Language.* TOEFL Research Reports, Report 1. Princeton, N.J.: Educational Testing Service, 1977.

Clark, John L. D., ed. *Direct Testing of Speaking Proficiency: Theory and Practice.* Princeton: Educational Testing Service, 1978.

Clark, Mark A. and Burdell, Linda. "Shades of Meaning: Syntactic and Semantic Parameters of Cloze Test Responses." In H.D. Brown, C.A. Yorio, and R.H. Crymes, eds. *On TESOL '77: Teaching and Learning English as a Second Language.* Washington, D.C.: TESOL, 1977, 131–143.

Cohen, Andrew D. "English Language Placement Testing: Separating Foreign English from Minority English." In R. Crymes and W.E. Norris, eds. *On TESOL '74.* Washington, D.C.: TESOL, 1975a, 189–199.

Cohen, Andrew D. "Error Correction and the Training of Language Teachers." *The Modern Language Journal,* 1975b, *59* (8), 414–422.

Cohen, Andrew D. *A Sociolinguistic Approach to Bilingual Education.* Rowley, Mass.: Newbury House, 1975c.

Cohen, Andrew D. "The Sociolinguistic Assessment of Speaking Skills in a Bilingual Education Program." In L. Palmer and B. Spolsky, eds. *Papers on Language Testing 1967–1974.* Washington, D.C.: Teachers of English to Speakers of Other Languages, 1975d, 172–186.

Cohen, Andrew D. "Successful Second-Language Speakers: A Review of Research Literature." *Balshanut Shimushit,* 1977, *1,* III–XII, ERIC ED 142 085.

Cohen, Andrew D. and Robbins, Margaret. "Toward Assessing Interlanguage Performance: The Relationship between Selected Errors, Learners' Characteristics, and Learners' Explanations." *Language Learning,* 1976, *26* (1), 45–66.

Cohen, Andrew D. and Aphek, Edna. *Easifying Second Language Learning.* A report financed by the Jacob Hiatt Institute, Jerusalem. ERIC ED 163 753. May 1979.

Cohen, Andrew D. and Fine, Jonathan. "Reading History in English: Discourse Analysis and the Experiences of Natives and Non-Native Readers." *Working Papers on Bilingualism,* 1978, *16,* 55–74.

Cohen, Andrew D. and Olshtain, Elite. "Developing a Measure of Sociocultural Competence: The Case of Apology." Jerusalem: Centre for Applied Linguistics, Hebrew University, 1980.

Cooper, Robert L. and Fishman, Joshua A. "A Study of Language Attitudes." In J.A. Fishman, R.L. Cooper, and A.W. Conrad, *The Spread of English.* Rowley, Mass.: Newbury House, 1977, 239–276.

Corder, S. Pit. "Error Analysis." In J.P.B. Allen and S.P. Corder, eds. *Techniques in Applied Linguistics.* London. Oxford University Press, 1974, 122–154.

Coulthard, Malcolm. *An Introduction to Discourse Analysis.* London: Longman, 1977.

Cowan, J. Ronyane. "Reading, Perceptual Strategies and Contrastive Analysis." *Language Learning,* 1976, *26* (1), 95–109.

Curran, Charles A. *Counseling-Learning in Second Languages.* Apple River, Ill.: Apple River Press, 1976.

Dailey, John T. *Language Facility Test, Test Administrator's Manual.* Alexandria, Va.: The Allington Corporation, 801 N. Pitt St. 701, 1968.

Darnell, Donald K. *The Development of an English Language Proficiency Test of Foreign Students, Using a Clozentropy Procedure.* Final Report. Colorado University, Boulder. ERIC ED 024 039, 1968.

DeAvila, Edward A. and Duncan, Sharon E. "Research on Cognitive Styles with Language Minority Children: Summary of Pilot Study Design and Data Analysis." Austin, Texas: Southwest Educational Development Laboratory, 1978.

Dobson, Barbara K. "Student-Generated Distractors in ESL Tests." In R. Crymes and W.E. Norris, eds. *On TESOL 74.* Washington, D.C.: TESOL, 1974, 181–188.

Dubin, Fraida and Margol, Myrna. *It's Time to Talk.* Englewood Cliffs, N.J.: Prentice-Hall, 1977.

Ebel, Robert L. *Measuring Educational Achievement.* Englewood Cliffs, N.J.: Prentice-Hall, 1965.

Fraser, Bruce. "Research in Pragmatics in Second Language Acquisition: The State of the Art." Boston: School of Education, Boston University, 1979.

Gardner, Richard C. and Lambert, Wallace E. *Attitudes and Motivation in Second-Language Learning.* Rowley, Mass.: Newbury House, 1972.

Gattegno, Caleb. *Teaching Foreign Language in Schools: The Silent Way.* New York: Educational Solutions, 80 Fifth Ave., N.Y. 10011, 1972.

George H. V. *Common Errors in Language Learning: Insights from English.* Rowley, Mass.: Newbury House, 1972.

Goodrich, Hubbard C. "Distractor Efficiency in Foreign Language Testing." *TESOL Quarterly,* 1977, *11* (1), 69–78.

Gorman, Thomas P. "The Teaching of Composition." In M. Celce-Murcia and L. McIntosh, eds. *An Introduction to Teaching English as a Second or Foreign Language.* Rowley, Mass.: Newbury House, 1979, 189–202.

Green, John A. *Teacher-Made Tests.* 2d ed. New York: Harper & Row, 1975.

Gregory, M. "Aspects of Varieties Differentiation." *Journal of Linguistics,* 1967, *3,* 177–198.

Hanzeli, Victor E. "Cloze Tests in French as a Foreign Language: Error Analysis." In E.J. Brière and F.B. Hinofotis, eds. *Concepts in Language Testing: Some Recent Studies.* Washington, D.C.: TESOL, 1979, 3–11.

Harris, David P. *Testing English as a Second Language.* New York: McGraw-Hill, 1969.

Haskell, John F. "Using Cloze to Select Reading Material." *TESOL Newsletter,* 1976, *10* (1), 15–16.

Heaton, James B. *Writing English Language Tests.* London: Longman, 1975.

Henning, Grant H. "Measurement of Psychological Differentiation and Linguistic Variation: A Study of the Relationship Between Field-Dependence-Independence, Locus of Control, Hemispheric Localization, and Variations in the Occurrence of Syntactic Classes in Written Language." Ph.D. Dissertation, University of California, Los Angeles, 1978.

Hinofotis, Frances A. B. "An Investigation of the Concurrent Validity of Cloze Testing as a Measure of Overall Proficiency in English as a Second Language." Ph.D. Dissertation, Southern Illinois University, 1976.

Hosenfeld, Carol. "The New Student Role: Individual Differences and Implications for Instruction." In G.A. Jarvis, ed. *Perspective: A New Freedom.* Skokie, Ill.: National Textbook Company, 1975, 129–167.

Hosenfeld, Carol. "Learning about Learning: Discovering Our Students' Strategies." *Foreign Language Annals,* 1976, *9* (2), 117–129.

Hosenfeld, Carol. "A Preliminary Investigation of the Reading Strategies of Successful and Nonsuccessful Second Language Learners." *System,* 1977, *5* (2), 110–123.

Hosenfeld, Carol. "Cindy: A Learner in Today's Foreign Language Classroom." In W.C. Born, ed. *The Learner in Today's Environment.* Montpelier, Vt.: Capital City Press, 1979.

Hughes, Arthur G. "Conventional Cloze as a Measure of Oral Ability." Reading, U.K.: Department of Linguistic Science, University of Reading, 1978.

Ilyin, Donna. "Structure Placement Tests for Adults in English-Second-Language Programs in California." *TESOL Quarterly,* 1970, *4* (4), 323–330.

Ilyin, Donna. *Oral Interview Test.* Revised Edition. Rowley, Mass.: Newbury House, 1976.

Ilyin, Donna. "Placement—Where?" Revised manuscript, Alemany Community College, 750 Eddy St., San Francisco, Calif. 94109, 1979.

Ilyin, Donna. *A Technical Manual for ELSA (English Language Skills Assessment).* Rowley, Mass.: Newbury House, forthcoming.

Ingram, Elisabeth. "Language Testing." In J.P.B. Allen and S. Pit Corder, eds. *Techniques in Applied Linguistics.* London: Oxford University Press, 1974, 313–343.

Jakobovits, Leon A. *Foreign Language Learning: A Psycholinguistic Analysis of the Issues.* Rowley, Mass.: Newbury House, 1970.

Jakobovits, Leon A. and Gordon, Barbara. *The Context of Foreign Language Teaching.* Rowley, Mass.: Newbury House, 1974.

Jenks, Frederick L. "Homework Assignments in the E.S.L. Class that Work." *TESOL Newsletter,* 1979, *13* (4), 11–12, 22.

Jones, Randall L. "Testing: A Vital Connection." In J.K. Phillips, ed. *The Language Connection: From the Classroom to the World.* Skokie, Ill.: National Textbook Company, 1977, 237–265.

Jonz, Jon. "Improving on the Basic Egg: The M-C Cloze." *Language Learning,* 1976, *26* (2), 255–265.

Kato, Hiroki. "Some Thoughts on Oral Examinations for Advanced Students in Japanese." *System,* 1977, *5* (3), 181–186.

Key, Mary R. *Nonverbal Communication: A Research Guide and Bibliography.* Metuchen, N.J.: Scarecrow Press, 1977.

Kirn, Harriet E. "The Effect of Practice on Performance on Dictations and Cloze Tests." M.A. Thesis, ESL Section, Department of English, University of California, Los Angeles, 1972.

Kleinmann, Howard H. "Avoidance Behavior in Adult Second Language Acquisition." *Language Learning,* 1977, *27* (1), 93–107.

Knapp, Donald. "A Focused, Efficient Method to Relate Composition Correction to Teaching Aims." In H.B. Allen and R.N. Campbell, eds. *Teaching English as a Second Language.* New York: McGraw-Hill, 1972, 213–221.

Knapp, Donald. "The Utility of Oral Reading in Teaching ESL." *TESOL Newsletter,* 1978, *12* (3), 27.

Krashen, Stephen D. "Some Issues Relating to the Monitor Model." In H.D. Brown, C.A. Yorio, and R.H. Crymes, eds. *On TESOL '77. Teaching and Learning English as a Second Language: Trends in Research and Practice.* Washington, D.C.: TESOL, 1977, 148–158.

Krashen, Stephen D. "The Theoretical and Practical Relevance of Simple Codes in Second Language Acquisition." Los Angeles: Department of Linguistics, University of Southern California, 1978.

Krypsin, William J. and Feldhusen, John F. *Developing Classroom Tests: A Guide for Writing and Evaluating Test Items.* Minneapolis, Minn.: Burgess, 1974.

Lado, Robert. *Language Testing.* London: Longmans, 1961.

Lapkin, Sharon and Swain, Merrill. "The Use of English and French Cloze Tests in a Bilingual Education Program Evaluation: Validity and Error Analysis." *Language Learning,* 1977, *27* (2), 279–314.

Laufer, Batia. "An Experiment in Teaching Reading Comprehension with Written Answers in the Mother Tongue." *System,* 1978, *6* (1), 11–20.

Lehtonen, Jaakko. "Problems of Measuring Fluency and Normal Rate of Speech." Jyväskylä, Finland: Department of Phonetics and Linguistics, University of Jyväskylä, 1978.

Levenston, E. A. "Aspects of Testing the Oral Proficiency of Adult Immigrants to Canada." In L. Palmer and B. Spolsky, eds. *Papers on Language Testing 1967–1974.* Washington, D.C.: TESOL, 1975, 66–74.

Levenston, E. A. "Error Analysis of Free Composition: The Theory and the Practice." *Indian Journal of Applied Linguistics,* 1978, *4* (1), 1–11.

Lewis, Heloise E. "Learning Spanish in Jamaica: A Study of Errors Caused by Language Transfer in a Diglossic Situation." Ph.D. Dissertation, University of Toronto, 1974.

Lindvall, C. Mauritz and Nitko, Anthony J. *Measuring Pupil Achievement and Aptitude.* 2d ed. New York: Harcourt Brace Jovanovich, 1975.

MacKay, Robert. "Standardized Tests: Objective/Objectified Measures of 'Competence'." In A.V. Cicourel et al. *Language Use and School Performance.* New York: Academic Press, 1974, 218–247.

Madsen, Harold. "Laboratory Versus Traditional Methods of Teaching Remedial English: An Analysis and Experiment." M.A. Thesis, University of Utah, 1960.

Marshall, Jon Clark and Hales, Loyde W. *Classroom Test Construction.* Reading, Mass.: Addison-Wesley, 1971.

McKay, Sandy. "Syllabuses: Structural, Situational, Notional." *TESOL Newsletter,* 1978, *12* (5), 11.

Mehan, Hugh. "Ethnomethodology and Education." In D. O'Shea, ed. *The Sociology of the School and Schooling.* Washington, D.C.: National Institute of Education, 1974.

Moy, Raymond H. "The Effect of Vocabulary Clues, Content Familiarity and Proficiency on Cloze Scores." M.A. Thesis, ESL Section, Department of English, University of California, Los Angeles, 1975.

Mullen, Karen A. "Rater Reliability and Oral Proficiency Evaluations." In J.E. Redden, ed. *Proceedings of the First International Conference on Frontiers in Language Proficiency and Dominance Testing.* Occasional Papers on Linguistics No. 1, Southern Illinois University, Carbondale, Ill., 1977, 133–142.

Munby, John. *Communicative Syllabus Design.* Cambridge, England: Cambridge University Press, 1978a.

Munby, John. "A Problem-Solving Approach to the Development of Reading Comprehension Skills." Presentation at the Regional University Teachers of English in Israel (UTELI) Meeting (January 25, 1978) Jerusalem, Israel. 1978b.

Munby, John. "Teaching Intensive Reading Skills." In R. Mackay, B. Barkman, and R.R Jordan, eds. *Reading in a Second Language.* Rowley, Mass.: Newbury House, 1979, 142–158.

Murakami, Ken. "A Language Aptitude Test for the Japanese (GTT)." *System,* 1974, *2* (3) 31–47.

Naiman, N., Fröhlich, M., Stern, H. H., and Todesco, A. *The Good Language Learner.* Research in Education Series No. 7. Toronto, Ontario: Modern Language Centre, Ontario Institute for Studies in Education, 1978.

Nation, I. S. P. "Translation and the Teaching of Meaning: Some Techniques." *English Language Teaching Journal,* 1978, *32* (3), 171–175.

Nilsen, Don L. F. and Nilsen, Alleen Pace. *Pronunciation Contrasts in English.* New York: Regents, 1971.

Nir, Rafael and Cohen, Andrew D. "The Development of Placement Tests for Learners of Hebrew." *Balshanut Shimushit* (J. of Israeli Applied Ling. Assoc.), *3*, in press.

Nir, Rafael and Blum-Kulka, Shoshana. "The Study of Reading Comprehension Processes: A Multi-Level Analysis of Cloze Errors." *Studies in Education* (School of Education, Haifa University), *26*, in press. (In Hebrew)

Oller, John W., Jr. "Dictation as a Test of ESL Proficiency." In H.B. Allen and R.N. Campbell, eds. *Teaching English as a Second Language: A Book of Readings.* New York: McGraw-Hill, 1972, 346–366.

Oller, John W., Jr. "Cloze Tests of Second Language Proficiency and What They Measure." *Language Learning,* 1973, *23* (1), 105–118.

Oller, John W., Jr. "Cloze, Discourse, and Approximations to English." In M.K. Burt and H.C. Dulay, eds. *On TESOL '75: New Directions in Second Language Learning, Teaching and Bilingual Education,* Washington, D.C.: TESOL, 1975, 345–355.

Oller, John W., Jr. "Language Testing." In R. Wardhaugh and H.D. Brown, eds. *A Survey of Applied Linguistics.* Ann Arbor: University of Michigan Press, 1976, 275–300.

Oller, John W., Jr. *Language Tests at School: A Pragmatic Approach,* London: Longman, 1979.

Oller, John W., Jr., Bowen, D., Dien, T.T., and Mason, V.W. "Cloze Tests in English, Thai, and Vietnamese: Native and Non-Native Performance." *Language Learning,* 1972, *22* (1), 1–16.

Oller, John W., Jr. and Richards, Jack D., eds. *Focus on the Learner: Pragmatic Perspectives for the Language Teacher.* Rowley, Mass.: Newbury House, 1973.

Ozete, Oscar. "The Cloze Procedure: A Modification." *Foreign Language Annals,* 1977, *10* (5), 565–568.

Pikulski, John J. and Pikulski, Edna C. "Cloze, Maze, and Teacher Judgment." *The Reading Teacher,* 1977, *30* (7), 766–770.

Pimsleur, Paul. "Testing Foreign Language Learning." In A. Valdman, ed. *Trends in Language Teaching.* New York: McGraw-Hill, 1966, 175–215.

Popham, W. James. *Criterion-Referenced Instruction.* Belmont, Calif.: Fearon, 1973.

Popham, W. James. *Criterion Referenced Measurement.* Englewood Cliffs, N.J.: Prentice-Hall, 1978.

Porter, Don. "Modified Cloze Procedure: A More Valid Reading Comprehension Test." *English Language Teaching,* 1976, *30* 151–155.

Ramírez, Manuel and Castañeda, Alfred. *Cultural Democracy, Bicognitive Development, and Education.* New York: Academic Press, 1974.

Rand, Earl. "The Effects of Test Length and Scoring Method on the Precision of Cloze Test Scores." *Workpapers in Teaching English as a Second Language,* 1978, *12,* University of California, Los Angeles, 62–71.

Rickard, Richard B. "Exploring Perceptual Strategies and Reading in a Second Language: Performance Differences between Speakers of Different Native Languages." *TESOL Quarterly,* 1979, *13* (4), 599–622.

Rigg, Pat. "Reading in ESL." In J.F. Fanselow and R.H. Crymes, eds. *On TESOL '76.* Washington, D.C.: TESOL, 1976, 203–210.

Rivers, Wilga M. *Teaching Foreign-Language Skills.* Chicago: The University of Chicago Press, 1968.

Rivers, Wilga M. and Temperley, Mary S. *A Practical Guide to the Teaching of English as a Second or Foreign Language.* New York: Oxford University Press, 1978.

Robbins, Margaret. "Error Explanations: A Procedure for Examining Written Interlanguage Performance." M.A. Thesis, ESL Section, Department of English, University of California, Los Angeles, 1977.

Rodríguez-Brown, Flora V. and Cohen, Andrew D. "Assessing Spanish Reading: Criterion-Referenced Testing." In A.D. Cohen, M. Bruck, and F.V. Rodríguez-Brown, *Evaluating Evaluation.* Bilingual Education Series: 6. Arlington, Va.: Center for Applied Linguistics, 1979, 23–39.

Roos-Wijgh, Ingrid F. "Testing Speaking Proficiency through Functional Dialogues." In J.L.D. Clark, ed. *Direct Testing of Speaking Proficiency.* Princeton: Educational Testing Service, 1978, 105–112.

Rossier, Robert E. "Extraversion-Introversion as a Significant Variable in the Learning of English as a Second Language." Ph.D. Dissertation, University of Southern California, 1975.

Rutherford, William E. *Modern English.* Vol. 1, 2d ed. New York: Harcourt Brace Jovanovich, 1975.

Sajavaara, Kari and Lehtonen, Jaakko. "Spoken Language and the Concept of Fluency." *Kielikeskusuutisia,* 1978, *1,* Language Centre for Finnish Universities, University of Jyväskylä, 23–57.

Savignon, Sandra J. *Communicative Competence: An Experiment in Foreign-Language Teaching.* Philadelphia: The Center for Curriculum Development, 1972.

Schlue, Karen M. "An Inside View of Interlanguage: Consulting the Adult Learner about the Second Language Acquisition Process." M.A. Thesis, University of California, Los Angeles, 1977.

Schulz, Renate A. "Discrete-Point versus Simulated Communication Testing in Foreign Languages." *Modern Language Journal,* 1977, *61* (3), 94–101.

Schulz, Renate A. and Bartz, Walter H. "Free to Communicate." In G.A. Jarvis, ed. *Perspective: A New Freedom.* Skokie, Ill.: National Textbook Company, 1975, 47–92.

Schumann, John H. and Stenson, Nancy, eds. *New Frontiers in Second Language Learning.* Rowley, Mass.: Newbury House, 1974.

Sharwood Smith, Mike. "Optimalizing Interlanguage Feedback to the Foreign Language Learner." Utrecht, Netherlands: Department of English, University of Utrecht, 1978.

Shaw, A. M. "Foreign-Language Syllabus Development: Some Recent Approaches." *Language Teaching and Linguistics: Abstracts,* 1977, *10* (4), 217–233.

Shohamy, Elana. "Investigation of the Concurrent Validity of the Oral Interview with Cloze Procedure for Measuring Proficiency in Hebrew as a Second Language." Ph.D. Dissertation, University of Minnesota, 1978.

Silverman, R. J., Noa, J. K., and Russell, R. H. *Oral Language Tests for Bilingual Students: An Evaluation of Language Dominance and Proficiency Instruments.* Portland, Ore.: Northwest Regional Educational Laboratory, 1976.

Smolinski, Lois K. "Foreign Language Aptitude in Children: An Investigation of Current Theory and Research and Interrelated Disciplines." M.A. Thesis, ESL Section, Department of English, University of California, Los Angeles, 1970.

Spolsky, Bernard. "Language Testing—The Problem of Validation." *TESOL Quarterly,* 1968, *2* (2), 88–94.

Stenson, Nancy. "Induced Errors." In J.H. Schumann and N. Stenson, eds. *New Frontiers in Second Language Learning.* Rowley, Mass.: Newbury House, 1974, 54–70.

Stevick, Earl W. *Memory, Meaning, and Method: Some Psychological Perspectives on Language Learning.* Rowley, Mass.: Newbury House, 1976.

Stockwell, Robert P., Bowen, J. Donald, and Martin, John W. *The Grammatical Structures of English and Spanish.* Chicago: University of Chicago, 1965.

Stolz, Walter and Bruck, Margaret. *A Project to Develop a Measure of English Language Proficiency.* Final Report to the National Center for Education Statistics under Contract 300-75-0253. Arlington, Va.: Center for Applied Linguistics, 1976.

Stubbs, Joseph B. and Tucker, G. Richard. "The Cloze Test as a Measure of English Proficiency." *The Modern Language Journal,* 1974, *58* (5–6), 239–241.

Tarone, E., Cohen, A. D., and Dumas, G. "A Closer Look at Some Interlangauge Terminology: A Framework for Communication Strategies." *Working Papers on Bilingualism,* 1976, *9,* 76–90.

Taylor, Wilson L. "Cloze Procedure: A New Tool for Measuring Readability." *Journalism Quarterly,* 1953, *30,* 414–438.

TESOL. "But How Can You Teach Them English If You Don't Speak Their Language . . ." *TESOL Newsletter,* 1978, *12* (3), 13.

Thorndike, Robert L. and Hagen, Elizabeth. *Measurement and Evaluation in Psychology and Education.* 3d ed. New York: John Wiley & Sons, 1969.

Tucker, G. R., Hamayan, E., and Genesee, F. H. "Affective, Cognitive and Social Factors in Second Language Acquisition," *Canadian Modern Language Review,* 1976, *32,* 214–226.

Ulijn, Jan. "An Integrated Model for First and Second Language Comprehension and Some Experimental Evidence about the Contrastive Analysis Hypothesis." *System,* 1977, 5 (3), 187–199.

Ulijn, J. M. and Kempen, G. A. M. "The Role of the First Language in Second Language Reading Comprehension–Some Experimental Evidence." In G. Nickel, ed. *Proceedings of the Fourth International Congress of Applied Linguistics.* vol. 1, Stuttgart: Hochschul-Verlag, 1976, 495–507.

Upshur, John A. "Functional Proficiency Theory and a Research Role for Language Tests." In E. J. Brière and F. B. Hinofotis, eds. *Concepts in Language Testing: Some Recent Studies.* Washington, D.C.: TESOL, 1979, 75–100.

Valdman, Albert. "Communicative Use of Language and Syllabus Design." *Foreign Language Annals,* 1978, *11* (5), 567–578.

Valette, Rebecca M. *Directions in Foreign Language Testing.* New York: Modern Language Association, 1969.

Valette, Rebecca M. *Modern Language Testing,* 2d ed. New York: Harcourt Brace Jovanovich, 1977.

Wick, John W. *Educational Measurement.* Columbus, Ohio: Charles Merrill, 1973.

Wilkins, David A. *Notional Syllabuses.* London: Oxford University Press, 1976.

Witbeck, Michael C. "Peer Correction Procedures for Intermediate and Advanced ESL Composition Lessons." *TESOL Quarterly,* 1976, *10* (3), 321–326.

Index